W9-CJN-952

i love cinnamon rolls!

Judith Fertig

i love cinnamon rolls!

Judith Fertig

Andrews McMeel
Publishing, LLC

Kansas City · Sydney · London

Andrews McMeel Publishing, LLC
an Andrews McMeel Universal company
1130 Walnut Street, Kansas City, Missouri 64106
www.andrewsmcmeel.com

12 13 14 15 SHO 10 9 8 7 6 5 4 3 2 1

ISBN: 978-1-4494-2069-7

Library of Congress Control Number:
2012931541

DAN TRINA JEAN JULIE BEN

Photography: Ben Pieper
        Food styling: Trina Kahl
            Assistance: Dan Trefz
                Art direction and design: Julie Barnes
                    Editorial: Jean Lucas

ATTENTION: SCHOOLS AND BUSINESSES Andrews McMeel books are available at
quantity discounts with bulk purchase for educational, business, or sales promotional
use. For information, please e-mail the Andrews McMeel Publishing Special Sales
Department: specialsales@amuniversal.com

Introduction

Chapter 1:
In the Dough

Chapter 2:
Easy Cinnamon
Rolls

Chapter 3:
Old-Fashioned
Cinnamon Rolls

Chapter 4:
No-Knead
Cinnamon Rolls

Chapter 5:
Thin Strudel
Dough Cinnamon
Rolls

Chapter 6:
Vegan Cinnamon
Rolls

Chapter 7:
Whole Wheat
Cinnamon Rolls

Chapter 8:
Gluten-Free
Cinnamon Rolls

Chapter 9:
Danish Pastries

Metric
Conversions and
Equivalents

Index

i love cinnamon rolls.
wholeheartedly.
passionately.
devotedly.
and i'm not alone.

If you do an Internet search for "cinnamon roll recipe," you get over *1.4 million* results. North Americans *crave* their cinnamon rolls, and the confection is also popular around the world. Swedes love their cinnamon rolls so much that they actually have a *kanelbullens dag*, or Cinnamon Roll Day, on October 4. In any language, however, cinnamon rolls translate into "delicious."

cinnamon roll	United States and Canada
cinnamon bun	United Kingdom, Canada, and Australia
franzbrotchen	Germany and Austria
kanelsnegle	Denmark
korvapuusti	Finland
kanelbullar	Sweden
skillingsbollen	Norway
pain or brioche à la canelle	France and Quebec

With renewed interest in all things bread—from no-knead to bread machine, vegan, and gluten-free bread-making techniques—the cinnamon roll continues to intrigue. With the mix-and-match possibilities among different doughs, fillings, and toppings, the cinnamon roll continues to satisfy our need for a signature dish. And with the stresses of modern life, the cinnamon roll continues to comfort. If you love cinnamon rolls, like I do, then you're reading the right book!

I Love Cinnamon Rolls! starts you at whatever level of expertise or special dietary need you have, from making cinnamon rolls from mixes, to using a bread machine, to learning a traditional kneaded dough recipe, trying the no-knead technique, making light and delicious whole grain, gluten-free, or vegan cinnamon rolls, or laminating a Danish pastry dough for that rich and buttery croissant effect.

So, let's get started. We've got so many cinnamon rolls to sample. . . .

the history of cinnamon rolls

Since Egyptian times, cinnamon has added a warm spiciness to foods, its aroma celebrated in the Hebrew Song of Solomon. In Europe and the Arab world during the Middle Ages, ground cinnamon most often flavored savory dishes such as stews and *bistiya*, a meat pie. During the eighteenth century, German, Austrian, and Scandinavian bakers started using cinnamon, often paired with cardamom, in yeast-risen baked goods. And when those people came to North America, the cinnamon roll came with them.

Today, cinnamon rolls have become the quintessential comfort food, served at school and church fund-raisers, in airports to harried travelers, at bed and breakfast inns, bakeries in small towns and big cities, and our home kitchens.

anatomy of a cinnamon roll

A signature cinnamon roll is greater than the sum of its parts. Each layer adds flavor, texture, color, and moisture.

the pan sauce

This is the sauce you put in the bottom of the baking pan. It forms a bed for the cinnamon rolls to bake upon, keeping them moist while adding flavor and color. The simplest pan "sauce" is cooking spray or softened butter. More complex pan sauces include granulated or brown sugar to help form a caramel, fruit juices, nuts, crispy bacon, apples, toffee bits, or orange zest.

the dough

A cinnamon roll dough needs to be sweet and tender, yet sturdy enough to stand up to both a filling and a frosting, glaze, or inverted pan sauce. All eight doughs in this book accomplish that deliciously.

the filling

You have to have cinnamon somewhere, and it's usually in the filling. But how you create that filling can vary. The most common type is the brush of butter on the dough, then a sprinkling of cinnamon sugar. But you can also have a more crumbly cinnamon streusel paired with fruit, sweet cheese, a pumpkin blend or cinnamon oil (because it's colorless) blended with snowy white flaked coconut.

the topping

Toppings for cinnamon rolls range from the European egg wash, plus sugar or nuts, to the American ooey-gooey frosting.

Egg wash An egg wash is a whole egg, egg white, or yolk beaten with a little water, then brushed on top of the roll for a shiny golden or clear finish.

Pearl sugar Small, white, irregular pieces of sugar on top of a cinnamon roll provide a crunchy, sweet first bite.

Glaze This thin, translucent sweet finish is brushed on cinnamon rolls after they've baked. Basically, a glaze consists of confectioners' sugar, a liquid, and flavoring.

Icing This solidly white, somewhat thicker finish is meant to be piped, swirled, or drizzled decoratively on top of a just-baked cinnamon roll. An icing also consists of confectioners' sugar, a liquid, and flavoring.

Frosting The thickest topping is a spreadable frosting. Basically, a frosting is confectioners' sugar combined with butter and/or cream cheese and flavoring.

the cinnamon r

On the Shelf

You'll find many of these products in the baking or natural foods aisles at the grocery store. Find specialty flours from the Bob's Red Mill and Hodgson Mill brands, or at kingarthur.com. Use the freshest cinnamon and other spices for the best flavor, from spice houses like McCormick, Pioneer, Tone's, or penzeys.com.

Flours All-purpose (bleached or unbleached), bread flour, whole wheat, and gluten-free flours (brown rice, sorghum, millet, garbanzo bean, soy, cornstarch, potato, etc.)

Hot roll mix

Instant or bread machine yeast Store in the freezer after opening.

Vital wheat gluten (for whole wheat rolls)

Xanthan gum (for gluten-free rolls)

Salt Kosher or table salt

Chocolate Unsweetened cocoa powder, semisweet chocolate chips, Mexican chocolate tablets, chopped dark chocolate

Sweeteners Granulated sugar, light and dark brown sugar, raw sugar or date sugar, honey, maple syrup, agave nectar

Spices Cinnamon, allspice, green cardamom, ground ancho or chipotle chile, ground cloves, nutmeg, ground black pepper, Szechuan pepper

Coffee Fresh brewed and instant, or instant espresso powder

Flavor extracts Vanilla, rose water, cinnamon oil

Fresh Ingredients

Dairy Products Whole milk, buttermilk, sour cream, butter, cream cheese

Large eggs (or powdered egg replacer for vegan rolls)

Vegan Products Almond, soy, or rice milk. Buttery sticks. Powdered egg replacer.

Fresh Foods Apples, citrus fruits, fruit juices, gingerroot, pears, rose petals

Varieties of Cinnamon

Ground from the inner bark of shrubby trees that grow in tropical southeastern Asia—especially Vietnam, China, Ceylon, India, and Indonesia—cinnamon is available in several different varieties. When the bark is harvested and dried, it curls into quills, known as "stick cinnamon." Stick cinnamon is then ground into the spice we love. Like coffee beans grown in different regions, cinnamon from certain tropical locales can also have different characteristics.

Vietnamese or Saigon	The boldest, spiciest, sweetest cinnamon with the darkest color.
China	Bold, spicy, and strong, with a reddish brown cast.
Indonesian	Sweet and mellow; lighter reddish brown. Grocery store variety.
Ceylon	Known as "true cinnamon," palest in color, slightly citrus in flavor.

There's also more to cinnamon than love at first bite. Studies show that both the aroma and flavor of cinnamon perk us up and enhance brain function. No wonder we like to start the day—or revive in the afternoon—with a cinnamon roll!

an overview of
step by step

Measuring the flour

Scoop the flour from the bag or canister with one measuring cup, then dump it in another to measure. Skim the excess flour off the top with your finger or a knife, then add the flour to the bowl or the bread pan of an automatic bread machine.

Working with instant or bread machine yeast

Instant or bread machine yeast has a very fine granule that allows you to stir it into the flour without proofing it (sprinkling it over warm water until it bubbles up) first, saving you a step.

Warming the liquid ingredients

Heating the milk, butter, sugar, and salt together to a warm (110°F/43°C) temperature helps the yeast work more quickly. If you're not sure how hot the liquid is, insert an instant-read thermometer into it. At 130°F/55°C, yeast stops working, so make sure your liquid ingredients do not reach that high. After the liquid ingredients have warmed, whisk in the eggs.

Mixing the dough

Pour the warmed liquid ingredients into the flour and yeast. Use the paddle attachment on a stand mixer or a wooden spoon if you're mixing by hand. Blend it all together until you have a moist, soft, and somewhat slack dough that is still sticky.

Kneading

Kneading helps activate the gluten in the flour to trap the carbon dioxide released when the yeast starts working, and that process causes the dough to rise. Change the paddle attachment for the dough hook on a stand mixer or simply transfer the dough to a floured surface and knead by hand.

To knead by hand, dust the dough, then press it into an oval. With the heel or knuckles of your hand, press the oval all over. Fold the oval in half, turn the dough a quarter turn, then press it into an oval again and knead. Repeat the process. You usually knead only a few minutes for roll dough, until the dough firms up and bounces back when you press a finger into the dough.

You can omit this step for No-Knead and Gluten-Free Cinnamon Roll Doughs.

Rising

For an airy texture, the dough needs ample time to rise or sometimes just rest. Place the dough in an oiled bowl and cover with plastic wrap. Leave it to rise in a warm place until it has almost doubled in size, usually 45 to 60 minutes.

cinnamon rolls,

No-Knead Cinnamon Roll Dough will take 2 hours to rise at room temperature.

A "warm place" means about 85°F. To achieve this in a cool kitchen, turn the oven to 100°F with the door open. Place your covered bowl of dough on a shelf in the oven, and put a bowl of water next to it. Or make the dough using the dough cycle in a bread machine.

Room temperature means about 72°F. If your kitchen is cooler, the rising will take longer.

Laminating Danish Pastry Dough

Laminating a dough means adding butter layers. To do this, you add a crumbled mixture of cold butter and flour, much like pie pastry, to the Danish Pastry Dough (page 10) by rolling the mixture in, a little at a time. Keep laminated doughs cold so the butter layers stay intact. Use a marble pastry work surface, if possible, and work in a cool room. Only keep the dough at room temperature during the final rise.

Rolling out the dough

For most doughs in this book, you'll need to flour a surface— a kitchen counter, a large wooden cutting board, or a marble slab for pastry work. Flour the rolling pin. Roll the dough out to the dimensions required in the recipe, using a pastry brush to brush away excess flour.

Filling the dough

Usually you brush the dough with softened or melted butter, then sprinkle on a filling.

Forming the dough

To form the dough into a cylinder, start with either a long or a short end, as the recipe requires. Roll up the dough, jelly-roll fashion, keeping the cylinder as tight as possible as you roll, brushing off excess flour. After you've formed the dough into a cylinder, gently squeeze to elongate or compress to shorten the cylinder to the required length.

Cutting the dough

Use a serrated knife, a length of dental floss, or, in some cases, a pizza wheel to cut the dough into the required shapes.

Rising or resting

After you have filled and cut the rolls, there is a time for resting (the rolls don't rise much) or rising (increasing slightly or more in size), covered with tea towels.

>>>>

>>>>

Baking

Preheat the oven to the required temperature and bake the rolls as directed. Rolls that bake in a mass will take longer to get done in the middle of the pan than rolls baked individually. To test that the middle rolls in the pan are done, insert an instant-read thermometer in the center of a roll. If the roll registers 190°F or higher, the roll is done.

Pan Saucing, Egg Washing, Glazing, Icing, and Frosting the Rolls

Cinnamon rolls usually get some kind of finishing touch. With a thick pan sauce, the rolls bake in a sugary mixture that forms the topping when the rolls are inverted after baking. An egg wash is a thin brush of egg over an unbaked roll, sometimes with an added sprinkle of pearl or coarse sugar. Glazing involves brushing or drizzling a thin, translucent, sugary mixture over a baked roll. An icing is usually thicker and whiter than a glaze, while a frosting is thick and spreadable on a baked roll.

Storing and Freezing

Cinnamon rolls are best enjoyed the day they're made but can be stored in plastic storage bags and rewarmed in the microwave for a few seconds. Rolls made with Thin Strudel Dough (page 6) will keep for at least a week.

You can freeze prepared doughs, as well as formed but not yet baked rolls, in freezer bags or containers for up to 3 months. Freezing just puts the yeast in suspended animation for a while. The yeast will activate again when the dough or unbaked rolls come to room temperature. At that time, you can finish the recipe.

You can also freeze baked rolls—glazed but not frosted—in freezer bags or containers for up to 3 months. Let them come to room temperature, then wrap in aluminum foil and warm in a 350°F oven for 15 minutes. Spread newly made frosting on frozen, thawed, and warmed rolls for a gooey treat.

The eight cinnamon
roll doughs in this
chapter offer lots
of mix-and-match
possibilities for the
cinnamon roll baker.
No matter your
expertise or dietary
requirement—or the
type of cinnamon
roll you want to try—
there's a dough
for you.

chapter

1

in the dough

1 cup water

1/4 cup granulated sugar

4 tablespoons unsalted butter, softened

1 whole egg and 1 large egg yolk

1 (16-ounce) package hot roll mix

About 2/3 cup all-purpose flour for kneading and dusting

If you keep a package of hot roll mix on your pantry shelf (check the sell-by date), you can have homemade cinnamon rolls in about two hours. Hot roll mix combines a type of bread flour with dry milk, salt, and an instant yeast packet, so all you need to add is water, sugar, softened butter, and egg. You'll get a cinnamon roll with a moist, rich crumb. Try Coffee Lover's Cinnamon Monkey Bread Rolls (page 19), Szechuan Pepper Cinnamon Rolls with Fresh Ginger Glaze (page 20), or Rocky Road Cinnamon Rolls (page 17).

easy cinnamon roll dough

makes 6 jumbo, 12 large, 16 to 20 medium, or 48 mini rolls

1. In a 4-cup measuring cup, combine the water, sugar, and butter and whisk to blend. Microwave on High for 1 minute until warm, then whisk in the egg and egg yolk until the butter melts.

2. In a large bowl, empty the flour packet from the hot roll mix. Add the contents of the yeast packet and stir together with a fork. Stir in the liquid ingredients until you have a soft dough.

3. Flour your hands and a flat surface. Transfer the dough to the floured surface and form into a ball. Adding as little flour as necessary, knead the dough by pressing the dough into an oval, folding the oval in half, and pressing several times with your knuckles or heel of your hand. Turn the dough a quarter turn, press into an oval and repeat the process. Sprinkle with just enough flour to keep the dough from being sticky. When the dough is smooth and springs back when you press it with your finger, you've kneaded enough (3 to 5 minutes). Return the dough to the bowl. Let the dough rest for 15 minutes.

4. Proceed with a cinnamon roll recipe.

This classic dough makes a cinnamon roll with a sweet flavor and a feathery crumb. Instead of using a stand mixer, you can also make this dough by hand—see Easy Cinnamon Roll Dough (page 2) for mixing and kneading directions—or in a 2-pound capacity or larger bread machine (see variation).

traditional cinnamon roll dough

makes 6 jumbo, 12 large, 16 to 20 medium, or 48 mini rolls

1. In a 4-cup measuring cup, combine the milk, butter, sugar, and salt. Microwave on High for 1 minute or until warm. Whisk in the eggs.

2. Place the flour and yeast in the bowl of a stand mixer fitted with the paddle attachment. Add the liquid ingredients. Mix on low speed, stopping to scrape down the sides of the bowl from time to time, until the dough forms a soft mass and starts to pull away from the sides of the bowl, 5 to 6 minutes.

3. Remove the paddle attachment and switch to the dough hook. With the mixer on low, knead the dough with the dough hook. Sprinkle the dough with a tablespoon of flour, if necessary, to keep it from sticking to the sides of the bowl. When the dough is smooth, not sticky, and springs back when you press it with your finger, you've kneaded enough (4 to 6 minutes). Place the dough in a large, oiled mixing bowl, cover with a tea towel, and let rise in a warm place (about 85°F) for 45 to 60 minutes, or until it has almost doubled.

4. Proceed with a cinnamon roll recipe.

1 cup whole milk

4 tablespoons unsalted butter, softened

1/3 cup granulated sugar

1 teaspoon salt

2 large eggs

3 1/3 cups all-purpose flour, plus more for kneading and dusting

2 1/2 teaspoons instant or bread machine yeast

VARIATION: *For Traditional Cinnamon Roll Dough in the bread machine, place the liquid ingredients in the pan of the bread machine after step 1. Add the flour, then the yeast. Select Dough cycle, and press Start.*

VARIATION: *For Hot Cross Bun Dough, add 1 1/2 teaspoons ground cinnamon (or mixed spice: 3/4 teaspoon cinnamon, 1/2 teaspoon nutmeg, and 1/4 teaspoon allspice) and 2/3 cup dried currants in step 2 and proceed with the recipe.*

VARIATION: *For Honeybun Dough, use clover honey in place of sugar in step 1 and proceed with the recipe.*

On a scale of easiness, this one probably tops the list. Simply stir the ingredients together in a bowl, let the dough rise on the kitchen counter for 2 hours, then get rolling. Extra liquid takes the place of kneading. The dough is soft like a baby's skin and makes looser and less precisely shaped cinnamon rolls. When you taste Espresso-Chocolate Cinnamon Rolls with Cappuccino Drizzle (page 41) or Festive Cranberry-Orange Cinnamon Rolls (page 44), you'll know this dough is a winner.

no-knead cinnamon roll dough

makes 6 jumbo, 12 large, 16 to 20 medium, or 48 mini rolls

1/2 cup buttermilk

3/4 cup whole milk

4 tablespoons unsalted butter

1/2 cup granulated sugar

1 teaspoon salt

2 large eggs

3 1/4 cups all-purpose flour, plus more for dusting

1 tablespoon instant or bread machine yeast

1. In a 4-cup measuring cup, combine the buttermilk, milk, butter, sugar, and salt. Microwave on High for 1 1/2 minutes or until warm. Whisk in the eggs.

2. Mix the flour and yeast together in a bowl. Add the liquid ingredients and stir to combine. Beat for 40 strokes, scraping the bottom and the sides of the bowl, until the dough forms a lumpy, sticky mass.

3. Cover with plastic wrap and let rise in a warm place (about 85°F) for 2 hours or until the dough has risen to about 2 inches under the rim of the bowl and has a sponge-like appearance.

4. Proceed with a cinnamon roll recipe.

VARIATION: *For No-Knead Pumpkin Cinnamon Roll Dough, use 3/4 cup pureed cooked or canned pumpkin, 1/2 cup buttermilk, and 1/4 cup whole milk in place of 1/2 cup buttermilk and 3/4 cup whole milk.*

1/4 cup whole milk

1/2 cup sour cream

1/2 cup unsalted butter, softened

2 tablespoons granulated sugar

1 teaspoon salt

2 large eggs

3 1/4 cups all-purpose flour, plus more for kneading

2 1/2 teaspoons instant or bread machine yeast

VARIATION: *For Thin and Rich Cinnamon Strudel Dough in the bread machine, place the liquid ingredients in the pan of the bread machine after step 1. Add the flour, then the yeast. Select Dough cycle, and press Start.*

This is the dough to make when you want thin, somewhat crispy layers in the Eastern European tradition of Cinnamon Rugelach (page 51). It also makes delicious Small Indulgence Cinnamon Rolls (page 58), Slavic Cinnamon-Walnut Twists (page 56), and Tarte Tatin Cinnamon Rolls with Créme Fraîche (page 52).

thin strudel dough

makes 6 jumbo, 12 large, 16 to 20 medium, or 48 mini rolls

1. In a 4-cup measuring cup, combine the milk, sour cream, butter, sugar, and salt. Microwave on High for 1 1/2 minutes or until warm. Whisk in the eggs.

2. Place the flour and yeast in the bowl of a stand mixer fitted with the paddle attachment. Add the liquid ingredients. Mix on low speed, stopping to scrape down the sides of the bowl from time to time, until the dough forms a soft ball and pulls away from the sides of the bowl, 5 to 6 minutes.

3. Remove the paddle attachment and switch to the dough hook. With the mixer on low, knead the dough with the dough hook. Sprinkle the dough with a tablespoon of flour from time to time to keep it from sticking to the sides of the bowl. When the dough is smooth, not sticky, and springs back when you press it with your finger, you've kneaded enough (3 to 5 minutes). Place the dough in a large, oiled mixing bowl, cover with plastic wrap, and let rise in a warm place (about 85°F) for 45 to 60 minutes, or until it has almost doubled.

4. Proceed with a cinnamon roll recipe.

Can you make a delicious cinnamon roll with no eggs and no dairy? Yes, indeed! Rolls made this way feature a feathery crumb and moist texture—all vegan. And the best part? No one will ever guess. Packaged, dried egg replacer can be found in the baking section at better grocery or health food stores.

vegan cinnamon roll dough

makes 6 jumbo, 12 large, 16 to 20 medium, or 48 mini rolls

1. In a 4-cup measuring cup, combine the water, soy milk, sugar, vegan buttery-flavored sticks, and salt. Microwave on High for 1 1/2 minutes or until warm. Whisk in the egg substitute.

2. Place the flour and yeast in the bowl of a stand mixer fitted with the paddle attachment. Add the liquid ingredients. Mix on low speed, stopping to scrape down the sides of the bowl from time to time, until the dough forms a soft mass and starts to pull away from the sides of the bowl, 5 to 6 minutes.

3. Remove the paddle attachment and switch to the dough hook. With the mixer on low, knead the dough with the dough hook. Sprinkle the dough with a tablespoon of flour, if necessary, to keep it from sticking to the sides of the bowl. When the dough is smooth, not sticky, and springs back when you press it with your finger, you've kneaded enough (3 to 5 minutes). Place the dough in a large, oiled mixing bowl, cover with plastic wrap, and let rise in a warm place (about 85°F) for 45 to 60 minutes, or until it has almost doubled.

4. Proceed with a cinnamon roll recipe.

1/4 cup water

3/4 cup soy, rice, or almond milk, preferably vanilla flavored

1/2 cup granulated sugar or date sugar

4 tablespoons vegan buttery-flavored sticks, such as Earth Balance, softened

1 1/2 teaspoons salt

1 tablespoon powdered egg substitute, such as Ener-g Egg Replacer

3 1/3 cups all-purpose flour, plus more for kneading

2 1/2 teaspoons instant or bread machine yeast

VARIATION: For Vegan Cinnamon Roll Dough in the bread machine, place the liquid ingredients in the bread pan, then add the flour and yeast. Select the Dough cycle, and press Start.

3/4 cup whole milk

1/4 cup honey or agave nectar

1/4 cup vegetable oil

1 teaspoon salt

2 large eggs, beaten

1 1/2 cups whole wheat flour

1 1/2 cups all-purpose flour, plus more for kneading

2 teaspoons vital wheat gluten or whole grain dough improver

2 1/2 teaspoons instant or bread machine yeast

VARIATION: For Vegan Whole Wheat Cinnamon Roll Dough, use almond, rice, or soy milk in place of whole milk. Use 1 tablespoon powdered egg replacer mixed with 1/4 cup water in place of the eggs.

VARIATION: For Whole Wheat Dough in the bread machine, place the liquid ingredients in the pan of the bread machine after step 1. Add the flours, vital wheat gluten, then the yeast. Select the Dough cycle, and press Start.

The addition of whole wheat flour gives these rolls a slightly more textured, nutty flavor. Let the dough sit for 30 minutes after mixing, as the whole wheat flour takes longer to absorb liquids. Vital wheat gluten or whole grain dough improver can be found in the baking section of better grocery stores that carry Bob's Red Mill products, or online at places like kingarthur.com.

whole wheat cinnamon roll dough

makes 6 jumbo, 12 large, 16 to 20 medium, or 48 mini rolls

1. In a 4-cup measuring cup, combine the milk, honey, vegetable oil, and salt. Microwave on High for 1 minute or until warm. Whisk in the eggs.

2. Place the flour, vital wheat gluten, and yeast in the bowl of a stand mixer fitted with the paddle attachment. Add the liquid ingredients. Mix on low speed, stopping to scrape down the sides of the bowl from time to time, until the dough forms a soft ball and pulls away from the sides of the bowl, 5 to 6 minutes.

3. Remove the paddle attachment and switch to the dough hook. With the mixer on low, knead the dough with the dough hook. Sprinkle the dough with a tablespoon of flour every minute or so to keep it from sticking to the sides of the bowl. When the dough is smooth, not sticky, and springs back when you press it with your finger, you've kneaded enough (3 to 5 minutes). Place the dough in a large, oiled mixing bowl, cover with plastic wrap, and let rise in a warm place (about 85°F) for 45 to 60 minutes, or until it has almost doubled.

4. Proceed with a cinnamon roll recipe.

You'll find the dry ingredients for this dough in the baking or health food section of the grocery store. Gluten-free doughs don't require needing, but they do need time to rise. This batter-like dough results in a moist, rich crumb.

gluten-free cinnamon roll dough

makes 12 to 16 medium rolls

1. In a 4-cup measuring cup, whisk the water, vinegar, applesauce, brown sugar, oil, and salt together. Microwave on High for 1 minute or until lukewarm. Whisk in the eggs.

2. In a large bowl, whisk together the rice flour, tapioca flour, chickpea flour, xanthan gum, and yeast until well combined. Add the applesauce mixture and stir together with a fork until you have a soft, thick, batter-like dough.

3. Transfer the dough to an oiled bowl. Cover with a tea towel and let rise in a warm place (about 85°F) for 45 to 60 minutes, or until it has almost doubled.

4. Proceed with a cinnamon roll recipe.

1/2 cup water

1 teaspoon cider vinegar

1 cup unsweetened, gluten-free applesauce

1/4 cup packed light brown sugar

1/4 cup vegetable oil

1 teaspoon salt

2 large eggs, lightly beaten, or equivalent egg substitute

3/4 cup stone-ground brown rice flour

3/4 cup tapioca flour or potato starch

3/4 cup chickpea (garbanzo bean) flour

1 tablespoon xanthan gum

1 tablespoon instant or bread machine yeast

VARIATION: For Danish Pastry Dough in the bread machine, place the liquid ingredients in the pan of the bread machine after step 2. Add the flour, then the yeast. Select Dough cycle, and press Start. When the cycle is finished, proceed with step 4.

Buttery, yeasty, and slightly sweet, true Danish pastry—like croissants—can be a revelation. You start out with the sweet yeast dough known as the *détrempe*, to which you add a butter layer, or *buerrage*, to create a laminated dough, or one in which layers of butter create rich flakiness during baking. Plan for at least 2 days to make Danish pastry: the first day to make the dough and let it chill; and the next day to form, rise, and bake the pastries. Keep this dough cold, so the butter layers stay intact, and work in a cool room.

danish pastry dough

makes 12 large or 16 to 20 medium rolls

1. For the *buerrage*, place the flour in a medium bowl. Using a pastry blender, cut in the butter until the mixture is the size of small peas or smaller. (Or place the flour and butter in the food processor and pulse until the butter is the size of small peas or smaller.) Do not overwork; you want the butter to stay cold and solid. Cover and refrigerate for at least 1 hour and up to 1 day before proceeding.

2. In a 4-cup measuring cup, whisk the milk, orange juice, sugar, and salt together and microwave on High for 30 seconds or until lukewarm, about 100°F. Whisk in the eggs.

3. Place the flour and yeast in the bowl of a stand mixer fitted with the paddle attachment. Add the liquid ingredients. Mix on low speed, stopping to scrape down the sides of the bowl from time to time, until the dough forms a soft ball and pulls away from the sides of the bowl, 5 to 6 minutes.

>>>>

4. Remove the paddle attachment and switch to the dough hook. With the mixer on low, knead the dough with the dough hook. Sprinkle the dough with a tablespoon of flour every minute or so, to keep it from sticking to the sides of the bowl. When the dough is smooth, not sticky, and springs back when you press it with your finger, you've kneaded enough (3 to 5 minutes). Place the dough in a large, oiled mixing bowl, cover with plastic wrap, and let rise in a warm place (about 85°F) for 45 to 60 minutes or until it has almost doubled.

5. To add the butter layer, punch down the dough and transfer it to a floured surface. Dust very lightly with flour. Flour your hands and the rolling pin. Working the dough as little as possible and adding flour as necessary, roll out the dough into an 18 by 12-inch rectangle, using a dough scraper and your hands to lift and help form the dough into an even rectangle. Sprinkle half the buerrage on the top two-thirds of the dough, leaving a 1 1/2-inch border on the right and left sides. With your hands, lightly press the buerrage into the dough so it will stick. Fold the bottom third of the dough up and over some of the filling, like a business letter. Fold the top third of the dough down so the filling is completely covered and you have a 6 by 12-inch rectangle. Use your hands to scoop up stray buerrage and tuck it back under the dough, and to help form the dough into an even rectangle. Turn the dough a quarter turn, lightly flouring under and on top of the dough as necessary, and roll out again into an 12 by 18-inch rectangle with the long sides on your right and left. Repeat the process with the remaining buerrage. Cover with plastic wrap and refrigerate for 30 minutes.

6. Roll out the dough into a rectangle and fold like a business letter two more times. Use your hands to help form the dough into an even 6 by 12-inch rectangle. Lightly flour any sticky places on the dough. The dough should feel firm all over, with flattened pieces of butter visible within the dough, but not at all sticky.

7. Wrap the dough with plastic wrap and refrigerate for at least 30 minutes or for up to 24 hours before using in a cinnamon roll recipe.

From start to finish, these wonderful cinnamon rolls with a soft, moist crumb take about 2 hours to make. They use ingredients you probably have on hand, plus a box of hot roll mix.

chapter

2

easy cinnamon rolls

Adapted from a recipe by Ree Drummond, "Pioneer Woman" blogger/cookbook author/food television star, these Oklahoma-style rolls get a final, generous glaze, subtly flavored with real maple syrup and brewed coffee.

yummy glazed cinnamon rolls

makes 9 large rolls

PAN SAUCE:

4 tablespoons unsalted butter, softened

2 teaspoons cinnamon

2 tablespoons granulated sugar

DOUGH:

Flour for dusting

1 recipe Easy Cinnamon Roll Dough (page 2)

FILLING:

1 cup packed dark brown sugar

2 1/2 tablespoons cinnamon

6 tablespoons unsalted butter, softened

COFFEE GLAZE:

2 cups confectioners' sugar

Pinch of salt

1 tablespoon whole milk

1 tablespoon unsalted butter, melted

2 tablespoons strong brewed coffee

1/2 tablespoon maple syrup

1. For the pan sauce, spread the butter in a 9 by 13-inch pan. Mix the cinnamon and sugar together in a small bowl and sprinkle it over the butter.

2. Transfer the dough to a floured surface. Roll out to a 16 by 20-inch rectangle.

3. For the filling, mix the brown sugar and cinnamon together in a bowl. Spread the dough with the butter and sprinkle with the cinnamon sugar. Starting with a short side, roll up and form into a tight 18-inch cylinder. Cut the cylinder into 9 slices. Place each slice, spiral side up, in the prepared pan. Cover with tea towels and let rise in a warm place until almost doubled, 30 to 45 minutes.

4. Preheat the oven to 375°F. Bake for 20 to 23 minutes or until the rolls have risen and browned.

5. For the glaze, whisk all the ingredients together in a medium bowl. Drizzle over the warm rolls.

Little chunks of caramelized pineapple flavor the pan sauce for these rolls, which becomes the topping when you invert the rolls after baking.

pineapple upside-down cinnamon rolls

makes 18 small rolls

1. For the pan sauce, melt the butter in a medium saucepan over medium-high heat. Stir in the brown sugar until it melts. Stir in the pineapple chunks and juice and cook until the sauce starts to bubble and thicken, about 3 minutes. Stir in the salt, remove from the heat, and divide the sauce between two 9-inch square pans. Set aside to cool for 15 minutes. Arrange half the cherries, cut side up, in the bottom of each prepared pan.

2. Transfer the dough to a floured surface and cut in half. Roll each half out to an 8 by 12-inch rectangle.

3. For the filling, combine the cinnamon and sugar in a bowl. Set aside. Spread each half rectangle of dough with half the melted butter and sprinkle with half the cinnamon sugar. Roll up the dough, starting with a short end, to form a tight 9-inch cylinder. Cut each cylinder into 9 slices. Place each slice, spiral side up, in a prepared pan. Cover with tea towels and let rise in a warm place until almost doubled, 45 to 60 minutes.

4. Preheat the oven to 375°F. Bake for 23 to 25 minutes or until the rolls have risen and browned. Transfer to a rack to cool for 5 minutes before inverting onto serving platters.

PAN SAUCE:

1/2 cup (1 stick) unsalted butter

2/3 cup packed light brown sugar

1 1/2 cups canned pineapple chunks (juice reserved)

1/4 cup reserved pineapple juice

1/8 teaspoon salt

9 maraschino cherries, cut in half

DOUGH:

Flour for dusting

1 recipe Easy Cinnamon Roll Dough (page 2)

CINNAMON FILLING:

2 tablespoons cinnamon

1/2 cup granulated sugar

4 tablespoons unsalted butter, melted

PAN SAUCE:

4 tablespoons unsalted butter

6 tablespoons packed light brown sugar

1/4 cup unsweetened apple cider or juice

1/8 teaspoon salt

2 slices bacon, cooked until crisp and crumbled

DOUGH:

Flour for dusting

1 recipe Easy Cinnamon Roll Dough (page 2)

CINNAMON FILLING:

1 tablespoon cinnamon

1/3 cup packed light brown sugar

2 tablespoons unsalted butter, melted

Bacon makes everything better, including cinnamon rolls! Choose bacon that's not very smoky and cook it very crisp, so it's like a crunchy nut in the pan sauce.

bacon-brown sugar cinnamon rolls

makes 9 medium rolls

1. For the pan sauce, melt the butter in a medium saucepan over medium-high heat. Stir in the brown sugar until it melts. Stir in the cider and cook until the sauce starts to bubble and thicken, about 2 minutes. Stir in the salt, remove from the heat, and pour into a 9-inch square baking pan. Cool for 15 minutes. Sprinkle the bacon over the pan sauce.

2. Transfer the dough to a floured surface. Roll out to an 8 by 12-inch rectangle.

3. For the filling, combine the cinnamon and sugar in a bowl. Spread the dough with the butter and sprinkle with the cinnamon sugar. Roll up the dough, starting with a short end, to form a tight 9-inch cylinder. Cut the cylinder into 9 slices. Place each slice, spiral side up, in the prepared pan. Cover with a tea towel and let rise in a warm place until almost doubled, 45 to 60 minutes.

4. Preheat the oven to 375°F. Bake for 23 to 25 minutes or until the rolls have risen and browned. Transfer to a rack to cool for 5 minutes before inverting onto a serving platter.

In 1929, William Dreyer named his new ice cream flavor after the stock market crash on Wall Street. If the combination of chocolate, nuts, and marshmallows is great in ice cream, another food we obsess about, it's also fabulous for a cinnamon roll.

rocky road cinnamon rolls

makes 12 large rolls

1. For the pan sauce, spread the butter in a 9 by 13-inch pan.

2. Transfer the dough to a floured surface and cut the dough in half. Roll each half out to an 8 by 12-inch rectangle.

3. For the filling, mix the brown sugar and cinnamon together in a bowl. Spread each dough rectangle with half the butter. Sprinkle with half the cinnamon sugar, along with half of the marshmallows and chocolate chips. Starting with short side, roll the dough up and form into a tight cylinder. Cut each cylinder into 6 slices and place, spiral side up, in the prepared pan. Cover with a tea towel and let rise in a warm place until almost doubled, 30 to 45 minutes.

4. Preheat the oven to 375°F. Bake for 20 to 23 minutes or until the rolls have risen and lightly browned. Let cool in the pan for 10 minutes on a wire rack.

5. For the glaze, whisk all ingredients together. Drizzle the glaze over the warm rolls.

PAN SAUCE:
2 tablespoons unsalted butter, softened

DOUGH:
Flour for dusting

1 recipe Easy Cinnamon Roll Dough (page 2)

ROCKY ROAD FILLING:
1 cup packed light brown sugar

2 tablespoons cinnamon

6 tablespoons unsalted butter, softened

3 cups miniature marshmallows

1/2 cup miniature chocolate chips

VANILLA GLAZE:
2 cups confectioners' sugar

2 tablespoons unsalted butter, softened

1 tablespoon whole milk

1 teaspoon vanilla extract

The flavors of coffee, sugar, and cinnamon combine in these wake-you-up rolls in pull-apart form. You simply dip pieces of dough into melted butter, then spicy sugar, and arrange them in a Bundt pan. A coffee glaze provides the sweet finish.

coffee lover's cinnamon monkey bread rolls

makes 16 medium rolls

1. For the pan sauce, spread the butter on the inside of a 12-inch Bundt pan and scatter with pecans.

2. For the filling, combine the sugar, cinnamon, and instant coffee granules in a small bowl. Have the melted butter ready in another bowl.

3. Transfer the dough to a floured surface. Cut the dough into 16 pieces. Dip each piece in melted butter and roll in the filling. Place in the prepared pan. Cover with a tea towel and let rise at room temperature until almost doubled, 30 to 45 minutes.

4. Preheat the oven to 375°F. Bake for 30 to 32 minutes or until risen and browned. When the rolls are done, let them rest in the pan for 1 minute. Then, loosen them from the sides of the pan and invert the rolls onto a serving plate.

5. For the glaze, combine all the ingredients in a small saucepan and bring to a boil over medium-high heat. Whisk until well blended and remove from the heat. Drizzle or brush the rolls with glaze.

PAN SAUCE:
2 tablespoons unsalted butter, softened

1 cup toasted, chopped pecans

COFFEE CINNAMON FILLING:
2/3 cup granulated sugar

2 teaspoons cinnamon

2 tablespoons instant coffee granules

6 tablespoons unsalted butter, melted

DOUGH:
Four for dusting

1 recipe Easy Cinnamon Roll Dough (page 2)

COFFEE GLAZE:
1/3 cup freshly brewed coffee

1 cup packed light brown sugar

4 tablespoons unsalted butter

Pinch of salt

PAN SAUCE:

4 tablespoons unsalted butter, softened

DOUGH:

Flour for dusting

1 recipe Easy Cinnamon Roll Dough (page 2)

FILLING:

1 cup packed dark brown sugar

2 tablespoons cinnamon

1 teaspoon ground Szechuan pepper

6 tablespoons unsalted butter, softened

FRESH GINGER GLAZE:

2 cups confectioners' sugar

2 tablespoons whole milk

1 tablespoon unsalted butter, melted

1 tablespoon finely grated fresh gingerroot

Cinnamon rolls with a taste of the Far East? Why not? Tropical cinnamon combined with lemony Szechuan pepper creates an intriguingly delicious filling that makes your tongue tingle a bit at the end of a bite. The fresh grated ginger in the glaze makes these little rolls even more irresistible. Enjoy these with a steaming cup of herbal or green tea.

szechuan pepper cinnamon rolls with fresh ginger glaze

makes 18 small rolls

1. For the pan sauce, spread the butter in the bottom of two 9 by 9-inch pans.

2. Cut the dough in half and transfer to a floured surface. Roll each half out to an 8 by 12-inch rectangle.

3. For the filling, mix the sugar, cinnamon, and Szechuan pepper in a medium bowl. Spread each dough rectangle with 3 tablespoons of the softened butter and sprinkle with half the filling. Starting with the 12-inch side, roll the dough up and form into a tight cylinder. Cut each cylinder into 9 slices and place, spiral side up, in the prepared pans. Cover loosely with plastic wrap and let rise in a warm place for 30 minutes.

4. Preheat the oven to 350°F. Bake for 23 to 25 minutes, or until the rolls have risen and browned.

5. For the glaze, whisk all ingredients together in a medium bowl. Drizzle over the warm rolls.

When most North Americans envision a cinnamon roll, these are the pastries. Soft and feathery-crumbed, assertively cinnamon-flavored, with a big sweet finish, these cinnamon rolls satisfy that craving.

3

old-fashioned cinnamon rolls

DOUGH:

Flour for dusting

1 recipe Traditional Cinnamon Roll Dough (page 3)

FILLING:

1 cup packed dark brown sugar

2 1/2 tablespoons cinnamon

4 tablespoons unsalted butter, softened

FROSTING:

1 (3-ounce) package cream cheese, softened

4 tablespoons unsalted butter, softened

1 1/2 cups confectioners' sugar

1/2 teaspoon vanilla extract

1/8 teaspoon salt

Ooey-gooeyness at its finest! With a feathery crumb, a sweet and cinnamon-y filling, and a creamy frosting, this roll could be a clone of the famous Cinnabon.

classic cinnamon rolls

makes 12 large rolls

1. For the pan sauce, spread the butter into the bottom of a 9 by 13-inch pan.

2. Transfer the dough to a floured surface and roll out to a 16 by 20-inch rectangle.

3. For the filling, combine the brown sugar and cinnamon in a bowl. Spread the dough with the butter and sprinkle with the cinnamon sugar. Starting with a shorter side, roll up the dough to form a tight 16-inch cylinder. Cut the cylinder into 12 rolls. Place in the prepared pan spiral side up. Cover with a tea towel and let rise in a warm place until almost doubled, 45 to 60 minutes.

4. Preheat the oven to 350°F. Bake for 15 to 17 minutes or until lightly browned on top.

5. For the frosting, blend all the ingredients in the bowl of a food processor until smooth. Spread the frosting over the warm rolls.

Bakeries throughout the Midwest sell *schnecken*, the German word for "snails" (referring to the spiral shape). In Cincinnati, Ohio, a loaf of *schnecken* is composed of three coils of cinnamon, sugar, and raisin-filled yeast dough, baked on a thick bed of softened butter sprinkled with sugar. They're only available at holiday time, unless you bake your own. Because it's very rich, it's often sliced for serving, and one loaf will easily serve about eight people.

schnecken

makes 6 jumbo rolls

1. For the pan sauce, spread half of the butter into the bottom of two 5 by 9 by 3-inch loaf pans. Cover the bottom entirely or the schnecken will stick. Sprinkle half the sugar and a very little pinch of salt over the butter in each pan.

2. Transfer the dough to a floured surface and roll out to a 12-inch square.

3. For the filling, combine the brown sugar and cinnamon in a small bowl. Spread the butter over the dough. Sprinkle with the cinnamon sugar and raisins. Pat the filling into the dough. Roll up the dough to form a tight 12-inch cylinder. Cut the dough into 6 slices. Arrange 3 slices, spiral side up, in the bottom of each prepared pan. Cover the pans with a tea towel and let rise in a warm place until almost doubled, 45 to 60 minutes

4. Preheat the oven to 350°F. Bake for 20 to 22 minutes or until lightly browned. Let cool for 1 minute, then invert onto serving platters. You can pull apart the rolls to serve them, or slice each loaf into smaller portions.

PAN SAUCE:

1 cup (2 sticks) unsalted butter, softened

1 cup granulated sugar

Pinch of salt

DOUGH:

Flour for dusting

1 recipe Traditional Cinnamon Roll Dough (page 3)

CINNAMON FILLING:

2/3 cup packed light brown sugar

2 teaspoons cinnamon

4 tablespoons unsalted butter, softened

1 cup raisins

1/2 cup packed dark brown sugar

1 tablespoon cinnamon

Pinch of salt

DOUGH:
Flour for dusting

1 recipe Honeybun Dough (variation, page 3)

Vegetable oil for brushing

With the flavor of honey in the dough and a final dusting of cinnamon sugar, these coiled doughnuts are an East Coast tradition. Instead of frying, this oven-baking technique makes a roll that's easier and just as tasty. Cinnamon sugar provides a sweet and spicy finish.

cinnamon honeybuns

makes 24 small rolls

1. Line two baking sheets with parchment paper. For the cinnamon sugar, combine the sugar, cinnamon, and salt in a bowl.

2. Transfer the dough to a floured surface and cut into 24 pieces. Roll each piece into a 12-inch rope. Form each rope into a coil and pinch closed. Place the honeybuns on the prepared baking sheets, cover with tea towels, and let rise in a warm place until almost doubled, 45 to 60 minutes.

3. Preheat the oven to 400°F. Brush the rolls with vegetable oil. Bake 12 to 14 minutes, or until the honeybuns are a medium brown. While still warm in the pan, sprinkle each honeybun with cinnamon sugar.

PAN SAUCE:

4 tablespoons unsalted butter, softened

DOUGH:

Flour for dusting

1 recipe Traditional Cinnamon Roll Dough (page 3)

SPICED ORANGE FILLING:

4 tablespoons unsalted butter, softened

2 teaspoons freshly grated orange zest

2/3 cup granulated sugar

2 teaspoons cinnamon

SWEET ORANGE DRIZZLE

1 1/2 cups confectioners' sugar

1 teaspoon freshly grated orange zest

1/4 cup freshly squeezed orange juice

You'll need about 3 medium oranges for this recipe, for the zest and juice in the filling and for the glaze. These rolls smell so fabulous that you'll be tempted to gobble them up before they've cooled.

orange cinnamon rolls with sweet orange drizzle

makes 18 small rolls

1. For the pan sauce, spread the butter into the bottom of two 9-inch square baking pans.

2. Transfer the dough to a floured surface. Cut the dough in half. Roll each half out to an 8 by 12-inch rectangle.

3. For the filling, combine the butter and orange zest in a small bowl. Combine the sugar and cinnamon in a separate bowl. Spread half the orange butter over each half of the dough and sprinkle each with half the cinnamon sugar. Roll up the dough and form into a tight 12-inch long cylinder. Cut each cylinder into 9 slices. Arrange the slices, spiral side up, in the prepared pans. Cover the pans with a tea towel and place in a warm place to rise until almost doubled, 45 to 60 minutes.

4. Preheat the oven to 350°F. Bake for 25 to 27 minutes, or until lightly browned.

5. For the drizzle, whisk all the ingredients together in a small bowl. Drizzle over the warm rolls.

Sometimes bigger is better. Although these are not as big as the dinner-plate-size rolls at Johnson's Corner in Loveland, Colorado, they certainly fill out a dessert plate. For fans of cinnamon rolls from WheatFields Bakery Café in Lawrence, Kansas; Machine Shed restaurants throughout Iowa, Wisconsin, and Minnesota; or excess in general— this is your roll. Frosting the rolls while still warm gives a happily gooey result.

big-as-a-plate cinnamon rolls with gooey frosting

makes 6 jumbo rolls

1. For the pan sauce, spread the butter into the bottom of a 9-inch square baking pan. Combine the cinnamon and sugar and sprinkle over the butter.

2. Transfer the dough to a floured surface. Roll out the dough to a 12 by 26-inch rectangle.

3. For the filling, combine the sugar and cinnamon. Spread the butter over the dough and sprinkle with the cinnamon sugar. Pat the filling into the dough. Roll up the dough, starting with a short end, and form the cylinder into a fat 12-inch cylinder. Cut the cylinder into 6 slices. Arrange the slices, spiral side up, in the prepared pan. Cover the pan with a tea towel and place in a warm place to rise until almost doubled, 45 to 60 minutes.

4. Preheat the oven to 350°F. Bake for 25 to 27 minutes or until risen and browned.

5. For the frosting, whisk all the ingredients together in a bowl until smooth. Spread over the warm rolls.

PAN SAUCE:

4 tablespoons unsalted butter, softened

2 teaspoons cinnamon

2 tablespoons granulated sugar

DOUGH:

Flour for dusting

1 recipe Traditional Cinnamon Roll Dough (page 3)

CINNAMON FILLING:

1 cup packed dark brown sugar

2 1/2 tablespoons cinnamon

6 tablespoons unsalted butter, softened

GOOEY FROSTING:

1 1/2 cups confectioners' sugar

4 tablespoons unsalted butter, softened

Pinch of salt

1 tablespoon whole milk

1 teaspoon vanilla extract

Known as *kanelbullar*, these petite rolls form their own topknot. They're crisper and spicier than their North American cousins, meant to be enjoyed with a cup of strong coffee for a mid-morning or afternoon break. Make these in two batches; keep half of the dough covered in the refrigerator, then let it come to room temperature to form into rolls and bake in your prettiest cupcake papers.

swedish cinnamon rolls

makes 48 mini rolls

1. Line 48 muffin cups with cupcake liners.

2. Transfer the dough to a floured surface. Cut the dough in fourths. Roll each fourth out to an 8 by 12-inch rectangle.

3. For the filling, combine the sugar, cinnamon, and cardamom in a small bowl. Brush a fourth of the butter over the dough and sprinkle with a fourth of the spice mixture.

4. Roll up the dough and form into a tight 12-inch long cylinder. Cut each cylinder into 12 slices. Place each slice, spiral side up, in a paper-lined muffin cup. Repeat with the remaining dough. Cover the pans with a tea towel and place in a warm place to rise until almost doubled, 45 to 60 minutes.

5. Brush the tops of the rolls with egg wash and sprinkle with pearl sugar.

6. Preheat the oven to 350°F. Bake for 12 to 14 minutes, or until lightly browned.

DOUGH:
Flour for dusting

1 recipe Traditional Cinnamon Roll Dough (page 3)

CINNAMON-CARDAMOM FILLING:
1/2 cup granulated sugar

1 tablespoon cinnamon

1 teaspoon cardamom

4 tablespoons unsalted butter, melted

EGG WASH:
2 large egg yolks, beaten with 2 teaspoons water

TOPPING:
3/4 cup Swedish pearl sugar or coarsely crushed sugar cubes

Mexican chocolate—a blend of chocolate, sugar, and cinnamon—can go grocery store or artisan. You can find Ibarra and Abuelita grocery store brands in the Hispanic drink aisle. Specialty chocolate makers Kakua in Mexico and Taza in Massachusetts make different varieties of Mexican chocolate, some with ground chiles added for a little extra zip. Mexican chocolate comes in 3-inch or so tablets that you must grate or coarsely chop to use in this recipe.

mexican chocolate cinnamon rolls

makes 24 small rolls

1. For the pan sauce, spread the butter into the bottom of two 9-inch square baking pans.

2. Transfer the dough to a floured surface. Cut in half. Roll each half to an 8 by 12-inch rectangle.

3. For the filling, mix the brown sugar, cinnamon, chile, and salt in a bowl. Spread each dough rectangle with half the butter. Sprinkle with half the filling and half the Mexican chocolate. Starting with a long end, roll up and form into a tight 12-inch cylinder. Cut each cylinder into 12 slices. Place each slice, spiral side up, in the prepared pans. Cover with tea towels and let rise in a warm place until almost doubled, 45 to 60 minutes.

4. Preheat the oven to 350°F. Bake for 12 to 14 minutes or until risen and browned. Cool completely.

5. For the icing, whisk all the ingredients together in a bowl until smooth. Drizzle the icing over the cooled rolls.

PAN SAUCE:

4 tablespoons butter, softened

DOUGH:

Flour for dusting

1 recipe Traditional Cinnamon Roll Dough (page 3)

CINNAMON-PEAR FILLING:

1/2 cup all-purpose flour

1/2 cup packed light or dark brown sugar

1/4 cup granulated sugar

2 teaspoons cinnamon

1/4 teaspoon salt

4 tablespoons unsalted butter, softened

1 large, ripe pear, peeled, cored, and finely chopped

WARM PEAR CARAMEL:

2/3 cup packed light or dark brown sugar

3 tablespoons cornstarch

2 cups pear nectar or apple cider

6 tablespoons heavy cream

3 tablespoons unsalted butter

1/4 teaspoon coarse kosher or sea salt or as desired

For a cold weather brunch—or breakfast for dinner— these rolls get a final drizzle of warm pear caramel. You can find bottled pear nectar in the health food section of better grocery stores.

cinnamon-spiced pear rolls with warm pear caramel

makes 12 large rolls

1. For the pan sauce, spread the butter into the bottom of a 10-inch springform pan.

2. Transfer the dough to a floured surface. Roll the dough out to a 10 by 12-inch rectangle.

3. For the filling, combine the flour, sugars, cinnamon, and salt in a medium bowl. Work in the butter with a fork or your fingers until the mixture forms crumbs. Dot the dough with the spice mixture and chopped pear. Pat the filling into the dough. Roll up the dough and form into a tight 12-inch cylinder. Cut the dough into 12 slices and place, spiral side up, in the prepared pan.

4. Preheat the oven to 350°F. Bake for 25 to 27 minutes, or until the rolls have risen and browned.

5. For the caramel sauce, whisk the brown sugar and cornstarch together in a large saucepan. Press out any lumps with your fingers. Stir in the pear nectar and cook over medium-high heat, whisking constantly, until large bubbles form around the perimeter of the pan and the sauce thickens, 10 to 12 minutes. Remove from the heat and whisk in the cream, butter, and salt until the butter melts. Drizzle over the rolls.

This centuries-old recipe is so popular we still sing about it in a nursery rhyme. The yeasty spice and dried fruit buns are eaten in England on Good Friday. This version features cinnamon in the dough, but feel free to use the traditional mixed spice combination of cinnamon with a little nutmeg and allspice, if you prefer.

cinnamon hot cross buns

makes 18 medium buns

1. Line a baking sheet with parchment paper.

2. Transfer the dough to a floured surface. Cut the dough into 18 pieces and form each piece into a ball. Place the pieces 1 inch apart on the prepared pan. Cover with a tea towel and let rise in a warm place until almost doubled, 45 to 60 minutes.

3. Brush the top of each roll with the egg wash.

4. Preheat the oven to 375°F. Bake for 20 to 22 minutes or until risen and browned.

5. For the icing, whisk all the ingredients together until smooth. Spoon the icing into a sealable plastic sandwich bag. Snip a corner from the bag and squeeze an icing cross onto each bun.

DOUGH:
Flour for dusting

1 recipe Hot Cross Bun Dough (variation, page 3)

EGG WASH:
1 large egg mixed with 1 teaspoon water

HOT CROSS BUN ICING:
2/3 cup confectioners' sugar

1 teaspoon vanilla extract

2 teaspoons milk

3/4 cup (1 1/2 sticks) unsalted butter

1 1/2 cups packed light brown sugar

1/3 cup clover honey

1/3 cup heavy cream

1/4 teaspoon kosher salt

1/2 cup toasted, chopped pecans

DOUGH:

Flour for dusting

1 recipe Traditional Cinnamon Roll Dough (page 3)

CINNAMON-PECAN FILLING:

1/4 cup granulated sugar

1/4 cup packed light brown sugar

2 teaspoons cinnamon

1/8 teaspoon salt

4 tablespoons unsalted butter, softened

1/2 cup toasted, chopped pecans

Sticky buns, beloved in New England, feature a gooey, caramelized pan sauce that forms the topping when a pan of rolls is inverted. Inspired by Joanne Chang's fabulous sticky buns at Flour Bakery and Café in Boston, these buns bake to a dark brown, glossy finish and are best served warm. To toast whole pecans, place them on a baking sheet at 350°F for 15 minutes, then chop.

new england sticky buns

makes 12 large buns

1. For the pan sauce, melt the butter in a saucepan over medium-high heat and whisk in the brown sugar until well combined but not smooth. Remove from the heat and whisk in the honey, cream, and salt until smooth. Let cool to room temperature, about 30 minutes, then pour and spread into a 9 by 13-inch pan. Scatter the pecans over the pan sauce.

2. Transfer the dough to a floured surface and roll to a 16 by 20-inch rectangle.

3. For the filling, combine the sugars, cinnamon, and salt. Spread the dough with the butter and sprinkle with the cinnamon sugar mixture, then the pecans. Starting with a short end, roll up and form into a tight 16-inch cylinder. Cut the cylinder into 12 slices. Place each slice, spiral side up, in the prepared pan. Cover with a tea towel and let rise in a warm place until almost doubled, 45 to 60 minutes.

4. Preheat the oven to 350°F. Bake for 22 to 25 minutes or until medium brown in the creases. Let cool in the pan for 20 minutes, then turn out each roll, one by one, onto a serving platter and top with pan sauce.

No kneading?
No problem! This
moister dough
forms looser, more
relaxed rolls that
taste just as
fabulous as the
traditional type.

chapter

4

no-knead
cinnamon rolls

PAN SAUCE:

4 tablespoons unsalted butter, melted

SWEET CHEESE FILLING:

12 ounces (about 1 1/2 cups) small-curd cottage cheese

1/4 cup heavy cream

1 tablespoon all-purpose flour

1/2 teaspoon salt

1/2 cup granulated sugar

2 large eggs, beaten

1 teaspoon vanilla extract

CINNAMON STREUSEL:

1/2 cup all-purpose flour

1/2 cup packed light or dark brown sugar

1/4 cup granulated sugar

2 teaspoons cinnamon

1/4 teaspoon salt

4 tablespoons unsalted butter, softened

DOUGH:

Flour for dusting

1 recipe No-Knead Cinnamon Roll Dough (page 5)

VANILLA GLAZE:

2 cups confectioners' sugar

1/4 cup milk

2 teaspoons vanilla extract

When I get a hankering for Graeter's muffin-size sweet rolls known as "crowns," I make these. Although primarily known for ice cream, this fourth-generation family business in Cincinnati, Ohio, also makes wonderful baked goods. They're so popular that Graeter's publishes a baking schedule, which you can check out online.

sweet cheese and cinnamon streusel crowns

makes 36 small crowns

1. For the pan sauce, brush the butter on the inside of six 6-cup muffin tins.

2. For the cheese filling, place all ingredients in a food processor or blender and puree until smooth. Set aside.

3. For the streusel, combine the flour, sugars, cinnamon, and salt in a medium bowl. Work in the butter with a fork or your fingers until the mixture forms crumbs. Set aside.

4. Transfer the dough to a floured surface. Flour your hands. With a floured dough scraper, cut the dough in fourths. Working the dough as little as possible and adding flour as necessary, roll each fourth into a 9-inch square. Cut the dough into 3-inch squares. Arrange each square in a prepared muffin tin. Place 2 teaspoons Sweet Cheese Filling and 2 teaspoons Cinnamon Streusel in each dough-lined muffin cup. Cover with tea towels and let rest at room temperature for 45 minutes.

5. Preheat the oven to 350°F. Bake for 15 to 17 minutes or until the crust has lightly browned and the filling is firm.

6. For the glaze, whisk all the ingredients together until smooth. Drizzle the glaze over the cooled rolls.

When you need a pick-me-up, these are the rolls for the job. Inside each sweet coil nestle chunks of espresso-flavored dark chocolate by Barry Callebaut. Buy the chocolate at specialty baking shops or at kingarthur.com.

espresso-chocolate cinnamon rolls with cappuccino drizzle

makes 24 small rolls

1. Line a large baking sheet with parchment paper.

2. Transfer the dough to a floured surface and dust very lightly with flour. Flour your hands. With a dough scraper, cut the dough in half. Working the dough as little as possible and adding flour as necessary, roll each half into an 8 by 12-inch rectangle.

3. For the filling, combine the brown sugar and cinnamon in a bowl. Spread half the butter over each dough rectangle and sprinkle with half the cinnamon sugar. Roll up the dough, starting with a long end, and form it into a 12-inch cylinder. Cut each cylinder into 12 slices. Place each slice, spiral side up, in the prepared pan. Cover with tea towels and let rest at room temperature for 45 minutes.

4. Preheat the oven to 350°F. Bake for 20 to 22 minutes or the rolls have risen and lightly browned.

5. For the glaze, whisk all the ingredients together until smooth. Drizzle the glaze over the cooled rolls. If you like, sprinkle chopped espresso chocolate chunks on each roll as a topping.

DOUGH:
Flour for dusting

1 recipe No-Knead Cinnamon Roll Dough (page 5)

FILLING:
2/3 cup packed light brown sugar

1 tablespoon cinnamon

4 tablespoons unsalted butter, softened

2/3 cup espresso chocolate chunks

CAPPUCCINO DRIZZLE:
1 1/2 cups confectioners' sugar

1 teaspoon cinnamon

2 tablespoons heavy cream, or more

2 tablespoons brewed coffee

TOPPING:
1/4 cup finely chopped espresso chocolate chunks, optional

Golden and delicious from pumpkin in the dough, these delectable rolls have all the flavor of autumn in an easy, no-knead recipe. No-knead dough is moister than my Traditional Cinnamon Roll Dough (page 3), so it won't form a tight cylinder.

no-knead pumpkin-cinnamon pullaparts

makes 18 medium rolls

1. For the pan sauce, spread the butter into two 8-inch round cake pans.

2. Transfer the dough to a floured surface and dust very lightly with flour. Flour your hands. With a floured dough scraper, cut the dough in half. Working the dough as little as possible and adding flour as necessary, roll each half into an 8 by 12-inch rectangle.

3. For the filling, combine the brown sugar and cinnamon in a bowl. Spread half the pumpkin butter over each dough rectangle and sprinkle with half the filling. Roll up the dough, starting with a short end, to form a 12-inch cylinder. Cut each cylinder into 9 slices. Place each slice, smooth side up, in a prepared pan, starting with the perimeter of the pan and moving toward the center. Cover with tea towels and let rest at room temperature for 45 minutes.

4. Preheat the oven to 350°F. Bake for 25 to 27 minutes or the rolls have risen and lightly browned.

5. For the glaze, whisk all the ingredients together until smooth. Drizzle the glaze over the cooled rolls.

PAN SAUCE:
4 tablespoons unsalted butter, softened

DOUGH:
Flour for dusting

1 recipe No-Knead Pumpkin Cinnamon Roll Dough (variation, page 5)

FILLING:
1/2 cup packed light brown sugar

2/3 cup spiced pumpkin or apple butter

2 teaspoons cinnamon

CINNAMON-CIDER GLAZE:
1 1/2 cups confectioners' sugar

1 teaspoon cinnamon

1 tablespoon unsalted butter

1 tablespoon whipping cream or whole milk

2 tablespoons apple cider or juice

Pinch of salt

PAN SAUCE:

4 tablespoons unsalted butter, softened

CRANBERRY-ORANGE FILLING:

2 (12-ounce) bags cranberries

1/2 cup orange juice

4 teaspoons cinnamon

1 cup granulated sugar

4 tablespoons unsalted butter, softened

DOUGH:

Flour for dusting

1 recipe No-Knead Cinnamon Roll Dough (page 5)

SWEET ORANGE GLAZE:

1 1/2 cups confectioners' sugar

1 teaspoon freshly grated orange zest

1/4 cup orange juice

Make, bake, and freeze these rolls for up to three months ahead of a holiday gathering. Let them come to room temperature, then wrap them in foil and warm in a 350°F oven for a sweet treat that's easy on the host.

festive cranberry-orange cinnamon rolls

makes 16 medium rolls

1. For the pan sauce, spread the butter into the bottom of two 9-inch square baking pans. For the filling, combine the cranberries, orange juice, cinnamon, and sugar in a large pot over medium-high heat. Bring to a boil and cook, stirring occasionally, until the cranberries soften, about 7 minutes. Cool to room temperature, about 15 minutes. Have the softened butter ready.

2. Transfer the dough to a floured surface and dust very lightly with flour. Flour your hands. With the dough scraper, cut the dough in half. Working the dough as little as possible and adding flour as necessary, roll each half into a 10 by 16-inch rectangle. Spread half the butter over each rectangle, then half the cranberry mixture. Roll up the dough, starting with a long end, and form into a 16-inch cylinder. Cut each cylinder into 8 slices. Place each slice, spiral side up, in the prepared pans. Cover with tea towels and let rest at room temperature for 45 minutes.

3. Preheat the oven to 350°F. Bake for 20 to 22 minutes or until the rolls have risen and lightly browned.

4. For the glaze, whisk all the ingredients together until smooth. Drizzle the glaze over the cooled rolls.

A little bit of cardamom adds an elusive and very classic Swedish flavor to this beautiful tea ring. The no-knead dough makes it less formal looking and more relaxed than with traditional dough, but every bit as delicious. The soft, rich dough needs gentle coaxing into shape, using both hands at times, but the flavor results are worth it.

cardamom- and cinnamon- scented swedish tea ring

makes 12 large rolls

1. Line a large baking sheet with parchment paper.

2. Transfer the dough to a floured surface and dust very lightly with flour. Flour your hands and the rolling pin. Working the dough as little as possible and adding flour as necessary, roll out the dough to a 12 by 22-inch rectangle.

3. For the filling, combine the sugar, cinnamon, and cardamom in a small bowl. Spread the dough with the butter and sprinkle with the filling. Roll up the dough, starting with a long end, and form into a 24-inch cylinder. Pinch the long seam closed. Bring the ends together to form a circle and pinch closed. Lightly flour any sticky places on the dough. The dough should feel soft and smooth all over, like a baby's skin, but not at all sticky.

4. Using a flexible cutting board, transfer the tea ring to the prepared baking sheet, seam side down. With kitchen shears, starting from the outer rim, cut diagonal slashes in the tea ring,

>>>>

DOUGH:
Flour for dusting

1 recipe No-Knead Cinnamon Roll Dough (page 5)

CINNAMON-CARDAMOM FILLING:
1/2 cup granulated sugar

1 tablespoon cinnamon

1 teaspoon cardamom

4 tablespoons unsalted butter, melted

6 tablespoons unsalted butter, softened

ALMOND GLAZE:
1 cup confectioners' sugar

1/4 cup whole milk, half and half, or heavy cream

1 teaspoon almond extract

GARNISH:
1 cup candied green cherries, optional

1 cup candied red cherries, optional

three-quarters of the way through the dough almost to the center of the ring, at 2-inch intervals. Gently fan the slices, going in the same direction, so the filling shows. Cover with a tea towel and let rest at room temperature for 45 minutes.

5. Preheat the oven to 350°F. Bake for 25 to 28 minutes or until risen and browned and an instant-read thermometer inserted in the center of the ring registers at least 190°F. Transfer to a wire rack to cool.

6. For the glaze, whisk all the ingredients together in a bowl. When the tea ring has cooled, drizzle with the glaze. Garnish with green and red candied cherries, if using.

Eastern European yeast-risen strudel dough, rich with butter and sour cream, can be rolled out very thinly. This makes it perfect for creating tight crescents and coils.

chapter

5

thin strudel dough cinnamon rolls

For people of Eastern European descent, "cinnamon roll" often connotes old-fashioned rugelach, the kind made with sour cream yeast dough that rolls out very thinly. *Rugelach* means "little twists" in Yiddish. The most famous American yeast dough rugelach come from Green Ackerman Bakery in Brooklyn, New York, and are inspired by the recipe of Chana Green, who came from a shtetl in Hungary. These tiny, toothsome, spicy little beauties keep well for a week or so and can be frozen for up to 3 months. Bags of these make great hostess or holiday gifts.

cinnamon rugelach

makes 64 rugelach

1. Line 2 baking sheets with parchment paper.

2. Transfer the dough to a floured surface and cut into fourths. Roll each fourth out to a circle 12-inches in diameter.

3. For the filling, combine all the ingredients in a bowl. Sprinkle each dough circle with one-quarter of the filling. Roll the filling into the dough. With a serrated knife or pizza wheel, cut each circle into 16 triangles. Starting at the wide end, roll each triangle up into a tight crescent and place on a prepared baking sheet about 1 inch apart. Cover with tea towels and let rest in a warm place for 45 minutes (they don't rise much). Reserve any filling that has collected after rolling.

4. Preheat the oven to 350°F. Brush each pastry with egg wash, then sprinkle on any remaining filling. Bake for 13 to 15 minutes or until lightly browned on top.

DOUGH:

Flour for dusting

1 recipe Thin Strudel Dough (page 6), used right after mixing

RUGELACH FILLING:

1/4 cup finely ground English walnuts

1/2 cup packed light brown sugar

1 tablespoon cinnamon

EGG WASH:

1 large egg beaten with 1 teaspoon water

CRÈME FRAÎCHE:

1/2 cup heavy cream

1/2 cup sour cream

TARTE TATIN PAN SAUCE:

3/4 cup (1 1/2 sticks) unsalted butter, softened

3/4 cup granulated sugar

4 large tart apples such as Granny Smith or Jonathan, peeled, cored, and finely chopped

Salt

DOUGH:

Flour for dusting

1 recipe Thin Strudel Dough (page 6), used right after mixing

CINNAMON FILLING:

4 tablespoons unsalted butter, softened

1/2 cup granulated sugar

1 tablespoon cinnamon

The aroma of these buttery, apple-scented rolls is as close to paradise as I can get sometimes. Like a classic Tarte Tatin, the upside-down French apple confection with a puff pastry crust, this bakes best in a cast-iron skillet.

tarte tatin cinnamon rolls with crème fraîche

makes 12 large rolls

1. For the Crème Fraîche, whisk together the ingredients in a bowl, cover with plastic wrap, and let it sit at room temperature for at least an hour and up to 24 hours.

2. For the pan sauce, heat the butter in a 10-inch (measured across the top) cast-iron skillet over medium-high heat. Stir in the sugar and apples and cook, stirring frequently, until the apples begin to brown and the sauce has thickened, 18 to 20 minutes. Remove from the heat and stir in salt.

3. Transfer the dough to a floured surface. Roll the dough out to a 12 by 18-inch rectangle.

4. For the filling, spread the butter over the dough. Combine the sugar and cinnamon in a bowl, then sprinkle over the dough. Pat the filling into the dough. Roll up the dough, starting with a long end, and form into a tight 18-inch cylinder. Cut the dough into 12 slices. Arrange the slices, spiral side up, on top of the apple pan sauce in the skillet.

5. Preheat the oven to 350°F. Bake for 20 to 22 minutes or until the rolls have risen and browned and the pan sauce is bubbling. Let cool for 1 minute, then carefully invert, wearing oven mitts, onto a serving platter. Serve each roll topped with pan sauce and a dollop of Crème Fraîche.

First there's the elusive flavor of rose, then the spiciness of cinnamon, and at the end, a faint heat from the pepper. In Tunisia and Morocco, a dried combination of rose, cinnamon, and black pepper is known as *baharat*. I've substituted a combination of fresh rose petals in the filling and rose water in the glaze. Snip off the white, bitter "heel" at the base of each petal before using. Enjoy these small crescents with a glass of Moroccan mint tea.

moroccan cinnamon rose petal crescents

makes 64 mini crescents

1. Line two large baking sheets with parchment paper.

2. Cut the dough into fourths. Roll out each fourth on a floured surface to a circle with a 12-inch diameter.

3. For the filling, combine the sugar, cinnamon, and black pepper in a bowl. Sprinkle each dough circle with one-quarter of the cinnamon sugar and scatter with one-quarter of the rose petals. Pat the filling into the dough. Cut each circle into 16 triangles. Starting at a wide end, roll up each triangle into a tight crescent. Place on the prepared baking sheets about 1 inch apart. Cover with tea towels and let rest in a warm place for 45 minutes (they don't rise much).

4. Preheat the oven to 350°F. Bake for 13 to 15 minutes or until lightly browned on top.

5. For the glaze, whisk all the ingredients and food coloring, if using, together in a bowl until smooth. Drizzle the glaze over the warm rolls.

DOUGH:
Flour for dusting

1 recipe Thin Strudel Dough (page 6), used right after mixing

MOROCCAN CINNAMON ROSE PETAL FILLING:
1/2 cup granulated sugar

1 tablespoon cinnamon

1 teaspoon finely ground black pepper

1 cup packed edible rose petals, white "heel" snipped off

ROSE GLAZE:
1 1/2 cups confectioners' sugar

3 to 4 tablespoons whole milk

1 teaspoon rose water

Tiny drop of pink food coloring, optional

CINNAMON-WALNUT FILLING:

3 cups shelled English walnut pieces

3/4 cup granulated sugar

1 1/2 tablespoons cinnamon

1 tablespoon vanilla extract

DOUGH:

Flour for dusting

1 recipe Thin Strudel Dough (page 6), used right after mixing

EGG WHITE WASH:

1 large egg white beaten with 1 teaspoon water

Povitica, meaning "swaddled" because of its many thin layers, is a popular festive Croatian bread. In this version, instead of rolling the filling into the dough, then forming it into a U-shape to bake in a loaf pan, you make bite-sized pastries. These keep for several weeks, so make a batch before a holiday, a vacation, or a family gathering. Remember to reserve 1 cup of the filling to also use as a topping.

slavic cinnamon-walnut twists

makes 64 mini twists

1. Line two large baking sheets with parchment paper.

2. For the filling, place the walnuts, sugar, cinnamon, and vanilla in a food processor or blender and pulse until the walnuts are very finely chopped. Reserve 1 cup of filling for a topping.

3. Cut the dough into fourths. Roll each fourth out on a floured surface to a circle with a 12-inch diameter. Sprinkle each circle with one-quarter of the filling. Pat the filling into the dough. Cut each circle into 16 triangles. Starting at the wide end, roll each triangle up into a tight crescent and place on a prepared baking sheet about 1 inch apart. Cover with tea towels and let rest in a warm place for 20 minutes (they don't really rise). Reserve any filling that has collected after rolling.

4. Preheat the oven to 350°F. Brush each pastry with egg white wash, then sprinkle with the remaining filling.

5. Bake for 13 to 15 minutes or until lightly browned on top.

A "crown" is baker's terminology for a miniature coffee-cake in the shape of a cupcake; the sweet dough forms a crown around the filling. The luscious blueberry filling and cinnamon streusel, with a final drizzle of Banana Glaze, make for a delicious way to rise and shine. Make these in batches if necessary; keep half of the dough covered in the refrigerator, then let come to room temperature to form into crowns.

cinnamon-blueberry crowns

makes 36 mini crowns

1. For the pan sauce, brush the inside of six 6-cup muffin tins with the melted butter. For the filling, combine all the ingredients in a saucepan and bring to a boil over medium-high heat. Cook, stirring, until the blueberries have softened, 3 to 5 minutes. Let cool to room temperature, about 15 minutes.

2. For the Cinnamon Streusel, combine all the ingredients in a medium bowl. Work in the butter with a fork or your fingers until the mixture forms crumbs. Set aside.

3. Transfer the dough to a floured surface. Cut the dough into fourths. Roll each fourth into a 9-inch square. Cut the dough into 3-inch squares. Fit each square into a prepared muffin cup. Place 2 teaspoons Blueberry Filling and 2 teaspoons Cinnamon Streusel in each dough-lined muffin cup. Cover with tea towels and let rest in a warm place for 20 minutes (they don't rise much).

4. Preheat the oven to 350°F. Bake for 15 to 17 minutes or until the crust has lightly browned and the filling is firm.

5. For the glaze, whisk all the ingredients together until smooth. Drizzle the glaze over the cooled rolls.

PAN SAUCE:
4 tablespoons unsalted butter, melted

BLUEBERRY FILLING:
3 cups fresh blueberries

1 cup blueberry preserves

1 tablespoon all-purpose flour

1/2 teaspoon lemon zest

CINNAMON STREUSEL:
1/4 cup all-purpose flour

1/4 cup packed light or dark brown sugar

2 tablespoons granulated sugar

1 teaspoon cinnamon

2 tablespoons unsalted butter, softened

1/8 teaspoon salt

DOUGH:
Flour for dusting

1 recipe Thin Strudel Dough (page 6), used right after mixing

BANANA GLAZE:
1 cup confectioners' sugar

I large ripe banana, peeled and mashed

1 teaspoon lemon juice

1 teaspoon vanilla extract

PAN SAUCE:

Cooking spray

CINNAMON-MOLASSES FILLING:

1/2 cup all-purpose flour

1/2 cup packed light brown sugar

1/4 cup granulated sugar

2 teaspoons cinnamon

1/4 teaspoon salt

1 large egg white

1 tablespoon molasses

4 tablespoons unsalted butter, softened

DOUGH:

Flour for dusting

1 recipe Thin Strudel Dough (page 6), used right after mixing

These little rolls always call to me when I'm at Whole Foods Market, so I figured out a way to make them. Tiny, slightly crispy, fully cinnamon flavored, and without glaze or frosting, they're the little black dress of cinnamon rolls. I like to dunk them in a skinny latte. Bake these in batches, then freeze rolls you don't eat right away for up to 3 months, so you always a have a treat on hand.

small indulgence cinnamon rolls

makes 48 mini rolls

1. For the pan sauce, spray the inside of four 12-cup mini muffin pans. For the filling, combine the flour, sugars, cinnamon, and salt in a medium bowl. Work in the egg white, molasses, and butter with a fork until the mixture forms moist crumbs. Set aside.

2. Cut the dough into fourths. Roll each fourth out on a floured surface to a 12-inch square. Gently spread each square with one-quarter of the topping. Roll up the dough and form into a tight cylinder. Cut the cylinder into 12 slices. Place each slice, spiral side up, in a prepared mini muffin cup. Let rise uncovered while the oven preheats.

3. Preheat the oven to 350°F. Bake for 15 to 17 minutes or until lightly browned on top.

If you want to live a vegan lifestyle, there is still a cinnamon roll for you. Using soy, almond, or rice milk; vegan buttery sticks; powdered egg substitute; and vegan cream cheese creates cinnamon rolls with all the deliciousness of traditional rolls.

vegan cinnamon rolls

4 tablespoons vegan buttery sticks, such as Earth Balance, softened

DOUGH:

Flour for dusting

1 recipe Vegan Cinnamon Roll Dough (page 7)

CINNAMON FILLING:

1 cup packed light brown sugar

2 1/2 tablespoons cinnamon

4 tablespoons vegan buttery sticks, such as Earth Balance, softened

VEGAN FROSTING:

1 (3-ounce) package vegan cream cheese, such as Tofutti, softened

4 tablespoons vegan buttery sticks, such as Earth Balance, softened

1 1/2 cups confectioners' sugar

1/2 teaspoon vanilla extract

I was, I admit, skeptical about vegan cinnamon rolls before I developed these. Decadent, feathery-crumbed, and cinnamon-y, these rolls have all the flavor and sweet indulgence of the classic version, but without the egg and dairy.

frosted vegan cinnamon rolls

makes 12 large rolls

1. For the pan sauce, spread the buttery stick in a 9 by 13-inch pan.

2. Transfer the dough to a floured surface. Roll out to a 16 by 20-inch rectangle.

3. For the filling, combine the brown sugar and cinnamon in a bowl. Spread the dough with the buttery stick and sprinkle with the cinnamon sugar. Starting with a short side, roll up the dough and form into a tight 16-inch cylinder. Cut the cylinder into 12 rolls. Place in the prepared pan, spiral side up. Cover with tea towels and let rise in a warm place until almost doubled, 45 to 60 minutes.

4. Preheat the oven to 350°F. Bake for 13 to 15 minutes or until risen and lightly browned.

5. For the frosting, blend all the ingredients in the bowl of a food processor or with a handheld mixer in a bowl. Spread the frosting over the warm rolls.

Bananas in the filling and in the sweet glaze keep the rolls moist, soft, and sweet.

going bananas vegan cinnamon rolls

makes 18 small rolls

1. For the pan sauce, spray a 9 by 13-inch baking pan with vegan cooking spray.

2. Transfer the dough to a floured surface. Roll the dough out to a 12 by 18-inch rectangle.

3. For the filling, mix the brown sugar and cinnamon together in a bowl. Spread the dough with the buttery stick and sprinkle with the cinnamon sugar and bananas. Starting with a long side, roll the dough up and form into a tight 18-inch cylinder. Cut the cylinder into 18 slices and place, spiral side up, in the prepared pan. Cover with a tea towel and let rise in a warm place until almost doubled, 45 to 60 minutes.

4. Preheat the oven to 350°F. Bake for 22 to 25 minutes or until the rolls have risen and browned.

5. For the glaze, whisk all the ingredients together in a medium bowl until smooth. Drizzle over the warm rolls.

PAN SAUCE:
Vegan cooking spray

DOUGH:
Flour for dusting

1 recipe Vegan Cinnamon Roll Dough (page 7)

CINNAMON FILLING:
1 cup packed dark brown sugar

2 1/2 tablespoons cinnamon

6 tablespoons vegan buttery-flavored sticks, such as Earth Balance, softened

2 large ripe-yet-firm bananas, peeled and cut into thin half-moons

BANANA GLAZE:
I large ripe banana, peeled and mashed

1 teaspoon vanilla extract

1 teaspoon lemon juice

1 cup confectioners' sugar

For a fabulous brunch, serve these with a mango, papaya, and blueberry compote. To keep the filling white, use cinnamon oil, available at the drugstore. Potently flavored cinnamon oil is used to help a toothache—and to make Italian cannoli filling spicy yet snowy white.

vegan coconut-cinnamon pullaparts with lime glaze

makes 18 small pullaparts

1. For the pan sauce, spray two 8-inch round cake pans with vegan cooking spray.

2. Transfer the dough to a floured surface and cut in half. Roll each half out to an 8 by 12-inch rectangle.

3. For the filling, place the cream cheese, egg substitute, water, sugar, flour, and cinnamon oil in the bowl of a food processor and process until smooth. Add the coconut and pulse just until blended. Spread each dough rectangle with half the filling. Starting with a long side, roll the dough up and form into a tight 12-inch cylinder. Cut each cylinder into 9 slices and place, smooth side up, in the prepared pan, starting with the perimeter and working toward the center of the pan. Cover with tea towels and let rise in a warm place until almost doubled, 45 to 60 minutes.

4. Preheat the oven to 350°F. Bake for 25 to 27 minutes or until the rolls have risen and browned.

5. For the glaze, whisk all the ingredients together in a medium bowl until smooth. Drizzle over the warm rolls.

PAN SAUCE:
Vegan cooking spray

DOUGH:
Flour for dusting

1 recipe Vegan Cinnamon Roll Dough (page 7)

COCONUT FILLING:
8 ounces vegan cream cheese, such as Tofutti, softened

1 1/2 teaspoons powdered egg substitute, such as Ener-g Egg Replacer

2 tablespoons water

1/4 cup granulated sugar

2 tablespoons all-purpose flour

1/2 teaspoon cinnamon oil, or 2 teaspoons cinnamon

1/2 cup sweetened flaked coconut

LIME GLAZE:
1 1/2 cups confectioners' sugar

1 to 2 tablespoons liquid non-dairy coffee creamer

1 teaspoon lime juice

1 teaspoon lime zest

Vegan cooking spray

SWEET POTATO FILLING:

1/4 cup plus 2 tablespoons water

1 1/2 tablespoons powdered egg substitute, such as Ener-g Egg Replacer

3/4 cup packed light brown sugar

1 1/2 cups canned and drained sweet potatoes, mashed

CINNAMON STREUSEL:

1/2 cup all-purpose flour

1/2 cup packed light or dark brown sugar

1/4 cup granulated sugar

2 teaspoons cinnamon

1/4 teaspoon salt

4 tablespoons vegan buttery sticks, such as Earth Balance, softened

DOUGH:

Flour for dusting

1 recipe Vegan Cinnamon Roll Dough (page 7)

BOURBON ICING:

1 1/3 cups confectioners' sugar

1 tablespoon vegan buttery stick, softened

1 tablespoon liquid nondairy coffee creamer

2 teaspoons bourbon

These moist rolls, baked in muffin tins, have a fabulous flavor and are as delicious for dessert as they are for breakfast. Bake these in batches, and sneak a roll or two as you go. For a nonalcoholic glaze, simply use more nondairy coffee creamer and 1 teaspoon rum extract in place of bourbon.

vegan sweet potato-cinnamon crowns with bourbon icing

makes 36 small rolls

1. For the pan sauce, spray the inside of six 6-cup muffin tins with vegan cooking spray. For the filling, whisk the water and egg substitute together until blended. Whisk in the brown sugar and sweet potato until smooth.

2. For the Cinnamon Streusel, combine the flour, sugars, cinnamon, and salt in a medium bowl. Work in the buttery stick with a fork or your fingers until the mixture forms crumbs.

3. Transfer the dough to a floured surface. Cut the dough into fourths. Roll each fourth to a 9-inch square. Cut the dough into 3-inch squares. Fit each square into a prepared muffin cup. Spoon in 1 tablespoon sweet potato filling and 2 teaspoons streusel. Cover with tea towels and let rest in a warm place until almost doubled, 45 to 60 minutes.

4. Preheat the oven to 350°F. Bake for 15 to 17 minutes or until the crust has lightly browned and the filling is firm.

5. For the icing, whisk all the ingredients together until smooth. Spoon the icing into a sealable plastic sandwich bag. Snip a corner from the bag and squeeze an icing zigzag across each crown.

The addition of whole wheat brings a nutty, mellow flavor and more texture to a cinnamon roll. Make sure to use vital wheat gluten or whole grain dough improver when making the dough, so the rolls rise high and light.

chapter

7

whole wheat cinnamon rolls

Rise and shine for a cold weather brunch dish that makes you happy! You will have some leftover pumpkin filling with this, but you can pour it into a buttered baking dish and bake it along with the rolls until a toothpick inserted in the center comes out clean. Bake these in batches, and nibble as you go.

whole wheat pumpkin-pecan cinnamon crowns

makes 36 small crowns

1. For the pan sauce, spray six 6-cup muffin tins with cooking spray or line with parchment paper. For the filling, whisk all the ingredients together until smooth.

2. For the streusel, combine the flour, sugars, cinnamon, salt, and pecans in a medium bowl. Work in the butter with a fork or your fingers until the mixture forms crumbs.

3. Transfer the dough to a floured surface. Cut the dough into fourths. Roll each fourth to a 9-inch square. Cut the dough into 3-inch squares. Arrange each square in a prepared muffin tin. Add 1 tablespoon pumpkin filling and 2 teaspoons streusel. Cover with tea towels and let rise in a warm place until almost doubled, 45 to 60 minutes.

4. Preheat the oven to 350°F. Bake for 15 to 17 minutes or until the crust has lightly browned and the filling is firm.

PAN SAUCE
2 tablesp
softene

1 large egg

CINNAMON-PECAN STREUSEL:

1/2 cup all-purpose flour

1/2 cup packed light or dark brown sugar

1/4 cup granulated sugar

2 teaspoons cinnamon

1/4 teaspoon salt

1/2 cup chopped pecans

4 tablespoons unsalted butter, softened

DOUGH:

Flour for dusting

1 recipe Whole Wheat Cinnamon Roll Dough (page 8)

...ons unsalted butter,

CARROT-CINNAMON FILLING:

1 cup grated carrots

1/4 cup packed light brown sugar

1 tablespoon cinnamon

1/3 cup raisins

2 tablespoons water

2 tablespoons unsalted butter, softened

DOUGH:

Flour for dusting

1 recipe Whole Wheat Cinnamon Roll Dough (page 8)

PINEAPPLE-CREAM CHEESE FROSTING:

1 (8-ounce) package cream cheese, softened

1 (8 to 8 1/2-ounce) can crushed pineapple, with juice

1/2 cup confectioners' sugar, or more as necessary

If you love carrot cake and you love cinnamon rolls, this recipe could become your favorite. I like to make two smaller pans and give one away or save it for later. For an oooey-gooey result, frost the rolls while they're still warm and eat them right away.

carrot cake cinnamon rolls with pineapple-cream cheese frosting

makes 12 large rolls

1. For the pan sauce, spread the butter in a 9 by 13-inch pan. For the filling, combine all the ingredients in a medium saucepan. Bring to a boil over medium-high heat. Remove from the heat and stir again. Cover and let come to room temperature, about 15 minutes. Have the softened butter ready.

2. Transfer the dough to a floured surface and sprinkle lightly with flour. Roll out the dough to a 12 by 16-inch rectangle. Spread the butter over the dough, then the cooled filling. Starting with a short end, roll up the dough and form into a tight 12-inch cylinder. Cut the cylinder into 12 slices. Place each slice, spiral side up, in the prepared pan. Cover with a tea towel and leave to rise in a warm place until almost doubled, 45 to 60 minutes.

3. Preheat the oven to 350°F. Bake for 18 to 20 minutes or until the rolls have risen and are just starting to brown. Let cool for 15 minutes.

4. For the frosting, mix all the ingredients together in a food processor or in a bowl with a hand mixer until smooth. Spread over the rolls.

Black walnuts and apple are a taste marriage made in heaven. Black walnuts can be difficult to pry out of their shells, so they're more readily available chopped. You'll find them in the baking aisle. You can also use pecans. To toast chopped black walnuts, place them on a baking sheet for 10 minutes in a 350°F oven.

whole wheat, black walnut, and apple cinnamon rolls

makes 18 medium rolls

1. For the pan sauce, spread the butter in two 9-inch square pans.

2. Transfer the dough to a floured surface and cut in half. Roll each half out to an 8 by 12-inch rectangle.

3. For the filling, mix the brown sugar and cinnamon in a bowl. Spread each dough rectangle with half the butter. Sprinkle each with half the cinnamon mixture, grated apple, and black walnuts. Press the filling into the dough. Starting with the short side, roll the dough up and form into a tight 12-inch cylinder. Cut each cylinder into 9 slices and place, spiral side up, in the prepared pans. Cover with tea towels and let rise in a warm place until almost doubled, 45 to 60 minutes.

4. Preheat the oven to 350°F. Bake for 23 to 25 minutes or until the rolls have risen and browned.

5. For the glaze, whisk all the ingredients together in a medium bowl. Drizzle over the warm rolls.

These rolls feature a feathery crumb, a deeply delicious cinnamon flavor, and an orange frosting that makes you feel happy.

orange frosted vegan whole wheat cinnamon rolls

makes 24 small rolls

1. For the pan sauce, spread the buttery sticks in two 9 by 13-inch pans.

2. Transfer the dough to a floured surface and cut in half. Roll each half out to an 8 by 12-inch rectangle.

3. For the filling, mix the brown sugar and cinnamon together in a bowl. Spread each dough rectangle with half the buttery stick and sprinkle with half the cinnamon sugar. Starting with the long side, roll the dough up and form into a tight 12-inch cylinder. Cut each cylinder into 12 slices and place, spiral side up, in the prepared pans. Cover with tea towels and let rise in a warm place until almost doubled, 45 to 60 minutes.

4. Preheat the oven to 350°F. Bake for 12 to 15 minutes or until the rolls have risen and browned. Let cool in the pan.

5. For the frosting, combine all the ingredients in the bowl of a food processor and process until smooth. Spread over the cooled rolls.

PAN SAUCE:
6 tablespoons vegan buttery-flavored sticks, such as Earth Balance, softened

DOUGH:
Flour for dusting

1 recipe Vegan Whole Wheat Cinnamon Roll Dough (variation, page 8)

FILLING:
1 cup packed dark brown sugar

2 1/2 tablespoons cinnamon

6 tablespoons vegan buttery-flavored sticks, such as Earth Balance, softened

VEGAN ORANGE FROSTING:
2 cups confectioners' sugar

1/4 cup vegan buttery-flavored sticks, such as Earth Balance, softened

1/3 cup vegan cream cheese, such as Tofutti, softened

1/4 cup orange juice

1 teaspoon grated orange zest

More and more gluten-free flours are available to bakers now, from brown rice and garbanzo bean flours to millet and sorghum flours. If other food sensitivities are a concern, then make these gluten-free rolls vegan as well by substituting almond, soy, or rice milk; egg substitute; vegan buttery sticks; and vegan cream cheese.

chapter 8

gluten-free cinnamon rolls

PAN SAUCE:

Gluten-free cooking spray

DOUGH:

Oil for rolling

1 recipe Gluten-Free Cinnamon Roll Dough (page 9)

CINNAMON FILLING:

1/2 cup packed dark brown sugar

1 1/2 tablespoons cinnamon

3 tablespoons unsalted butter or vegan buttery-flavored sticks, such as Earth Balance, softened

GLUTEN-FREE CREAM CHEESE FROSTING:

1/4 cup unsalted butter or vegan buttery-flavored sticks, such as Earth Balance, softened

1/3 cup cream cheese or vegan cream cheese, such as Tofutti, softened

1 teaspoon gluten-free vanilla extract

1 cup gluten-free confectioners' sugar

This gluten-free dough requires a different forming method than traditional wheat doughs. After baking, however, you'd be hard-pressed to tell the difference. Variation: For Vegan Gluten-Free Cinnamon Rolls, start with Vegan Gluten-Free Cinnamon Roll Dough (page 9), then use vegan buttery sticks, egg substitute, and vegan cream cheese for the filling and frosting.

frosted gluten-free cinnamon rolls

makes 12 medium rolls

1. For the pan sauce, spray two 6-cup muffin cups with gluten-free cooking spray.

2. Lightly oil a flexible cutting board. Transfer the dough to the cutting board. Oil a spatula or your hands and spread the dough into an 8 by 14-inch rectangle.

3. For the filling, combine the sugar and cinnamon in a small bowl. Gently spread the dough with the butter and sprinkle with the cinnamon sugar. Starting with a long side and using an oiled dough scraper, gently nudge or scrape the dough so it rolls over on itself again and again to form a loose 16-inch cylinder. This batter-like dough will not form a tight cylinder. With the dough scraper, gently cut the cylinder into 16 pieces. Place each piece, spiral side up, in a prepared muffin cup. Cover with tea towels and let rise in a warm place until almost doubled, 45 to 60 minutes.

4. Preheat the oven to 350°F. Bake for 15 to 18 minutes or until risen and lightly browned and an instant-read thermometer inserted in a roll registers 190°F. Transfer to a rack to cool.

5. For the frosting, blend all the ingredients together in a food processor or medium bowl until smooth. Spread over the cooled rolls.

This upside-down recipe, baked in a cast-iron skillet, makes its own glaze when you invert the pan onto a serving platter. Sorghum syrup, with a flavor similar to molasses, is a great sweetener for a gluten-free diet. Like real maple syrup, it's boiled down and processed in a mill that only makes the syrup, so there is no trace contamination from other products.

gluten-free skillet apple-cinnamon rolls

makes 8 jumbo rolls

1. For the pan sauce, heat the butter in a 10-inch (measured across the top) cast-iron skillet over medium-high heat. Stir in the sorghum and apples and cook, stirring frequently, until the apples begin to brown and the sauce has thickened, 18 to 20 minutes. Stir in salt.

2. Lightly spray a flexible cutting board. Transfer the dough to the cutting board. Spray a spatula or your hands and spread the dough into an 8 by 14-inch rectangle.

3. For the filling, combine the sugar and cinnamon in a small bowl. Gently spread the dough with the butter and sprinkle with the cinnamon sugar. Starting with a long side and using an oiled dough scraper, gently nudge or scrape the dough so it rolls over on itself again and again to form a loose 16-inch cylinder. The batter-like dough will not form a tight cylinder. With the dough scraper, gently cut the cylinder into 8 pieces. Place each piece, spiral side up, over the apple glaze in the skillet. Cover with tea towels and let rise in a warm place until almost doubled, 45 to 60 minutes.

4. Preheat the oven to 350°F. Bake for 25 to 27 minutes or until the rolls have risen and browned. Let cool for 1 minute, then invert onto a serving platter.

SORGHUM APPLE PAN SAUCE:

3/4 cup (1 1/2 sticks) unsalted butter or vegan buttery sticks, such as Earth Balance, softened

1/2 cup sorghum or maple syrup

4 large tart apples such as Granny Smith or Jonathan, peeled, cored, and finely chopped

Salt

DOUGH:

Oil for rolling

1 recipe Gluten-Free Cinnamon Roll Dough (page 9)

CINNAMON FILLING:

1/2 cup granulated sugar

1 tablespoon ground cinnamon

1 recipe Gluten-Free Cinnamon Roll Dough (page 9)

4 tablespoons unsalted butter or vegan buttery-flavored sticks, such as Earth Balance, softened

Banana and blueberry in the filling and sweet glaze keep the rolls moist, soft, and sweet.

gluten-free banana blueberry rolls

makes 12 large cinnamon rolls

1. For the pan sauce, spray two 6-cup muffin cups with gluten-free cooking spray.

2. Lightly oil a flexible cutting board. Transfer the dough to the cutting board. Oil a spatula or your hands and spread the dough into an 8 by 12-inch rectangle.

3. For the filling, mix the brown sugar, cinnamon, blueberry preserves, and lemon zest together in a bowl. Gently brush the melted butter over the dough, spread with the blueberry filling, and dot with the banana. Starting with the long side and using an oiled dough scraper, gently nudge or scrape the dough so it rolls over on itself again and again to form a 12-inch cylinder. With the dough scraper, gently cut the cylinder into 12 pieces. Place each piece, spiral side up, in a prepared muffin cup. Cover with tea towels and let rise in a warm place until almost doubled, 45 to 60 minutes.

3. Preheat the oven to 350°F. Bake for 15 to 18 minutes or until risen and lightly browned.

4. For the glaze, whisk all ingredients together in a medium bowl. Drizzle over the warm rolls.

PAN SAUCE:
Gluten-free cooking spray

DOUGH:
1 recipe Gluten-Free Cinnamon Roll Dough (page 9)

CINNAMON-BLUEBERRY FILLING:
1 cup packed dark brown sugar

2 tablespoons cinnamon

1 cup blueberry preserves

1/2 teaspoon lemon zest

3 tablespoons unsalted butter, melted

1 large ripe-yet-firm banana, peeled and cut into thin half-moons

BANANA GLAZE:
1 large ripe banana, peeled and mashed

1 teaspoon vanilla extract

1 teaspoon lemon juice

1 cup confectioners' sugar

PAN SAUCE:

Gluten-free cooking spray

1/2 cup chopped English walnuts

CINNAMON-WALNUT FILLING:

3/4 cup packed light brown sugar

1 1/2 tablespoons cinnamon

1/8 teaspoon salt

6 tablespoons unsalted butter, melted

DOUGH:

1 recipe Gluten-Free Cinnamon Roll Dough (page 9)

MAPLE DRIZZLE:

1/2 cup maple syrup

Pull these soft, fragrant, sticky, and spicy rolls apart and enjoy them for a special breakfast or brunch. Like all gluten-free cinnamon rolls, these are best served the day they're made.

gluten-free cinnamon-walnut monkey bread with maple drizzle

makes 16 medium pull-apart rolls

1. For the pan sauce, spray the inside of a 12-inch Bundt pan with gluten-free cooking spray and scatter with walnuts.

2. For the filling, combine the sugar, cinnamon, and salt in a small bowl. Dip an ice cream scoop or a 1/4-cup measure in the melted butter. Scoop out a portion of dough and gently toss it in the cinnamon mixture, then drop it in the prepared pan. Repeat the process 15 more times or until you have used all the dough. Drizzle any remaining butter over the dough and sprinkle with any remaining filling. Cover with a tea towel and let rise in a warm place until almost doubled, 45 to 60 minutes.

3. Preheat the oven to 350°F. Place the Bundt pan on a baking sheet. Bake for 30 to 32 minutes or until risen and browned.

4. For the drizzle, warm the maple syrup in the microwave. When the rolls are done, let them rest in the pan for 1 minute. Then, loosen the sides of the pan and invert the rolls onto a serving plate. Drizzle the rolls with the maple syrup.

Flaky and buttery like a croissant, but spicy like a cinnamon roll, these pastries are a gourmand's delight. Keep a batch of Danish Pastry Dough (page 10) in the freezer, so you can have fresh-baked rolls in no time.

g

danish pastries

Bear claws get their name from their resemblance to a bear's foot with its toes fanned out. A sprinkle of sugar makes the exterior crisp and sweet, in contrast to to the buttery, flaky, and sweetly cinnamon interior.

cinnamon bear claws

makes 16 medium bear claws

1. Line two baking sheets with parchment paper.

2. For the filling, mix all the ingredients together in a bowl until smooth.

3. Transfer the dough to a floured surface and cut in half. Rewrap the other half and return to the refrigerator. Roll out the dough to an 8 by 16-inch rectangle. The dough should feel cold, firm, and smooth all over, but not at all sticky. With a paring knife or pizza wheel, cut the dough into eight 4-inch squares. Place 2 teaspoons of cinnamon filling in the center of each square. Brush one side of each square with egg wash, then fold the opposite side over the filling, pressing the edges together to seal. Make three cuts on the folded side, almost but not quite to the seam side. Place the bear claws 2 inches apart on a prepared baking sheet. Gently spread the "toes" slightly. Repeat the process with the remaining dough. Cover lightly with tea towels and let rest at room temperature until slightly risen, about 2 hours.

4. Preheat the oven to 400°F. Brush the bear claws with egg wash. Bake for 10 to 12 minutes or until the rolls have puffed up and turned golden brown.

CINNAMON FILLING:

1/4 cup granulated sugar

1/4 cup packed dark brown sugar

1 tablespoon cinnamon

1/8 teaspoon salt

2 tablespoons unsalted butter, softened

DOUGH:

Flour for dusting

1 recipe Danish Pastry Dough (page 10), chilled

EGG WASH:

1 large egg yolk mixed with 1 teaspoon water

Cooking spray

DOUGH:
Flour for dusting

1 recipe Danish Pastry Dough (page 10), chilled

EGG WASH:
1 large egg yolk mixed with 1 teaspoon water

FILLING:
1/4 cup granulated sugar

1/4 cup packed light brown sugar

1 tablespoon cinnamon

1/2 cup small dark chocolate pieces or chocolate espresso chunks

CINNAMON-CRÈME FRAÎCHE ICING:
2 tablespoons sour cream

2 tablespoons half-and-half

1 cup confectioners' sugar

1/4 teaspoon cinnamon

Kerry Saretzky, creator of the food blog French Revolution Food, married her French heritage with her American upbringing with this recipe idea, which I have adapted here. For the best flavor, cut a dark chocolate bar into pieces or use espresso chocolate chunks from Barry Callebaut.

pain au chocolat cinnamon rolls with cinnamon-crème fraîche icing

makes 16 medium rolls

1. For the pan sauce, spray 16 muffin cups with cooking spray.

2. Transfer the dough to a floured surface and cut in half. Rewrap the other half and return to the refrigerator. Roll out the dough to an 8 by 12-inch rectangle. The dough should feel cold, firm, and smooth all over, but not at all sticky. Brush half the egg wash over the dough.

3. For the filling, combine the sugars and cinnamon in a small bowl. Sprinkle the dough with half the cinnamon sugar and half the chocolate pieces. Starting with a long side, roll up the dough into a tight 12-inch cylinder. Cut the cylinder into 8 slices. Place each slice in a muffin cup. Repeat the process with the remaining dough and filling. Cover lightly with tea towels and let rest at room temperature until slightly risen, about 2 hours.

4. Preheat the oven to 400°F. Bake for 10 to 12 minutes or until the rolls have puffed up and turned golden brown. Let cool for 10 minutes.

5. For the icing, whisk all the ingredients together in a medium bowl. Drizzle over the cooled rolls.

Known as *korvapuusti* or "slapped ears," these Finnish rolls are similar to Swedish Cinnamon Rolls (page 33) in flavor. To get their unique shape, however, you cut the dough cylinder into triangles instead of slices. More buttery, crisp, and spicy than sweet and gooey, these are delicious with freshly brewed coffee.

korvapuusti

makes 14 medium rolls

1. Line a baking sheet with parchment paper.

2. Transfer the dough to a floured surface and cut in half. Rewrap the other half and return to the refrigerator. Roll out the dough to an 8 by 14-inch rectangle. The dough should feel cold, firm, and smooth all over, but not at all sticky.

3. For the filling, combine the sugar, cinnamon, cardamon, and salt in a bowl. Brush half the melted butter over the dough and sprinkle with half the cinnamon sugar. Starting with a long side, roll up the dough into a tight 14-inch cylinder. Cut the cylinder into 7 triangles that are 2 inches wide at the top and 1 inch wide at the bottom. Place each roll in the prepared pan, smooth side up, about 2 inches apart. Repeat with the remaining dough and filling. Cover lightly with tea towels and let rest at room temperature until slightly risen, about 2 hours.

4. Preheat the oven to 400°F. Using the handle of a wooden spoon or the heel of your hand, squash each roll so the spiral interior comes out on each end. Brush the rolls with the egg wash and top with pearl sugar.

5. Bake for 10 to 12 minutes or until the rolls have puffed up and turned golden brown.

DOUGH:

Flour for dusting

1 recipe Danish Pastry Dough (page 10)

FILLING:

2/3 cup granulated sugar

2 tablespoons cinnamon

2 teaspoons green cardamom

1/8 teaspoon salt

4 tablespoons unsalted butter, melted

EGG WASH:

2 large egg yolks mixed with 2 teaspoons water

TOPPING:

1/2 cup pearl sugar or crushed sugar cubes

Flour for dusting

1 recipe Danish Pastry Dough
(page 10), chilled

FILLING:

2/3 cup granulated sugar

2 tablespoons cinnamon

1/8 teaspoon salt

4 tablespoons unsalted butter,
melted

EGG WASH:

2 large egg yolks mixed with
2 teaspoons water

These cinnamon rolls, or "Franz's rolls," are a breakfast specialty from Hamburg, Germany. They combine the buttery flakiness of a croissant with the sweet spiciness of a cinnamon roll.

franzbrotchen

makes 14 medium rolls

1. Line two baking sheets with parchment paper.

2. Transfer the dough to a floured surface and cut in half. Rewrap the other half and return to the refrigerator. Roll out the dough to an 8 by 14-inch rectangle. The dough should feel cold, firm, and smooth all over, but not at all sticky.

3. For the filling, combine the sugar, cinnamon, and salt in a bowl. Brush half the melted butter over the dough and sprinkle with half the sugar and cinnamon mixture. Starting with the long side, roll up the dough into a tight 14-inch cylinder. Cut the cylinder into 7 slices. Place each roll in a prepared pan, spiral side up, about 2 inches apart. Repeat with the remaining dough and filling. Cover lightly with tea towels and let rest at room temperature until slightly risen, about 2 hours.

4. Preheat the oven to 400°F. Using the handle of a wooden spoon or the heel of your hand, squash each roll so the spiral interior comes out on each end. Brush the rolls with the egg wash and top with pearl sugar.

5. Bake for 10 to 12 minutes or until the rolls have puffed up and turned golden brown.

pain au chocolat
cinnamon rolls
with cinnamon-
créme fraîche icing

franzbrotchen

Metric Conversion Formulas

To Convert	Multiply
Ounces to grams	Ounces by 28.35
Pounds to kilograms	Pounds by .454
Teaspoons to milliliters	Teaspoons by 4.93
Tablespoons to milliliters	Tablespoons by 14.79
Fluid ounces to milliliters	Fluid ounces by 29.57
Cups to milliliters	Cups by 236.59
Cups to liters	Cups by .236
Pints to liters	Pints by .473
Quarts to liters	Quarts by .946
Gallons to liters	Gallons by 3.785
Inches to centimeters	Inches by 2.54

Approximate Metric Equivalents

Length

1/8 inch	3 millimeters
1/4 inch	6 millimeters
1/2 inch	1 1/4 centimeters
1 inch	2 1/2 centimeters
2 inches	5 centimeters
2 1/2 inches	6 centimeters
4 inches	10 centimeters
5 inches	13 centimeters
6 inches	15 1/4 centimeters
12 inches (1 foot)	30 centimeters

Volume

1/4 teaspoon	1 milliliter
1/2 teaspoon	2.5 milliliters
3/4 teaspoon	4 milliliters
1 teaspoon	5 milliliters
1 1/4 teaspoons	6 milliliters
1 1/2 teaspoons	7.5 milliliters
1 3/4 teaspoons	8.5 milliliters
2 teaspoons	10 milliliters
1 tablespoon (1/2 fluid ounce)	15 milliliters
2 tablespoons (1 fluid ounce)	30 milliliters
1/4 cup	60 milliliters
1/3 cup	80 milliliters
1/2 cup (4 fluid ounces)	120 milliliters
2/3 cup	160 milliliters
3/4 cup	180 milliliters
1 cup (8 fluid ounces)	240 milliliters
1 1/4 cups	300 milliliters
1 1/2 cups (12 fluid ounces)	360 milliliters
1 2/3 cups	400 milliliters
2 cups (1 pint)	460 milliliters
3 cups	700 milliliters
4 cups (1 quart)	.95 liter
1 quart plus 1/4 cup	1 liter
4 quarts (1 gallon)	3.8 liters

S and equivalents

Weight

1/4 ounce	7 grams
1/2 ounce	14 grams
3/4 ounce	21 grams
1 ounce	28 grams
1 1/4 ounces	35 grams
1 1/2 ounces	42.5 grams
1 2/3 ounces	45 grams
2 ounces	57 grams
3 ounces	85 grams
4 ounces (1/4 pound)	113 grams
5 ounces	142 grams
6 ounces	170 grams
7 ounces	198 grams
8 ounces (1/2 pound)	227 grams
16 ounces (1 pound)	454 grams
35.25 ounces (2.2 pounds)	1 kilogram

Common Ingredients and Their Approximate Equivalents

1 cup all-purpose flour = 140 grams

1 stick butter (4 ounces • 1/2 cup • 8 tablespoons) = 110 grams

1 cup butter (8 ounces • 2 sticks • 16 tablespoons) = 220 grams

1 cup brown sugar, firmly packed = 225 grams

1 cup granulated sugar = 200 grams

Oven Temperatures

To convert Fahrenheit to Celsius, subtract 32 from Fahrenheit, multiply the result by 5, then divide by 9.

Description	Fahrenheit	Celsius	British Gas Mark
Very cool	200°	95°	0
Very cool	225°	110°	1/4
Very cool	250°	120°	1/2
Cool	275°	135°	1
Cool	300°	150°	2
Warm	325°	165°	3
Moderate	350°	175°	4
Moderately hot	375°	190°	5
Fairly hot	400°	200°	6
Hot	425°	220°	7
Very hot	450°	230°	8
Very hot	475°	245°	9

Information compiled from a variety of sources, including *Recipes into Type* by Joan Whitman and Dolores Simon (Newton, MA: Biscuit Books, 2000); *The New Food Lover's Companion* by Sharon Tyler Herbst (Hauppauge, NY: Barron's, 1995); and *Rosemary Brown's Big Kitchen Instruction Book* (Kansas City, MO: Andrews McMeel, 1998).

index

A

Abuelita brand Mexican chocolate, 34
alcohol, 64
apples
   Gluten Free Skillet Apple-Cinnamon Rolls, 75
   Sorghum Apple Pan Sauce, 75
   Tarte Tatin Cinnamon Rolls with Crème Fraîche, 52–53
   Whole Wheat, Black Walnut, and Apple Cinnamon Rolls, 70
apple cider, 16, 43, 70

B

Bacon-Brown Sugar Cinnamon Rolls, 16
baharat, 55
baking
   of dough, xviii
   steps for, xvi–xviii
bananas
   Gluten-Free Banana Blueberry Rolls, 76–77
   Going Bananas Vegan Cinnamon Rolls, 61
Barry Callebaut chocolate, 41, 82
Big-as-a-Plate Cinnamon Rolls with Gooey Frosting, 31
blueberries
   Cinnamon-Blueberry Crowns, 57
   Gluten-Free Banana Blueberry Rolls, 76–77
Bob's Red Mill, xiv, 8
bread machine
   Danish Pastry Dough, 10–12
   Thin and Rich Cinnamon Strudel Dough, 6
   Traditional Cinnamon Roll Dough, 3
   Vegan Cinnamon Roll Dough, 7
   Whole Wheat Cinnamon Roll Dough, 8
buerrage, 10–12

C

cardamom, 33
Cardamom- and Cinnamon-Scented Swedish Tea Ring, 46–48
Carrot Cake Cinnamon Rolls with Pineapple-Cream Cheese Frosting, 68–69
Ceylon cinnamon, xv
cheese. *See also* cream cheese
   Sweet Cheese and Cinnamon Streusel Crowns, 40
China cinnamon, xv
chocolate, xiv
   Espresso-Chocolate Cinnamon Rolls with Cappuccino Drizzle, 41
   Mexican Chocolate Cinnamon Rolls, 34–35
Pain au Chocolat Cinnamon Rolls with Cinnamon-Crème Fraîche Icing, 82, 85
Cinnamon. *See also specific varieties*
   baharat, 55
   cardamom with, x
   in savory dishes, x
   sticks of, xv
   varieties of, xv
Cinnamon Bear Claws, 80–81
Cinnamon Honeybuns, 28–29
Cinnamon Hot Cross Buns, 37
cinnamon oil, 63
cinnamon rolls. *See also* dough
   anatomy of, xii–xiii
   finishes for, xviii
   freezing of, xviii
   history of, x
   internationalization of, ix
   storage of, xviii
Cinnamon Rugelach, 50–51
Cinnamon-Blueberry Crowns, 57
Cinnamon-Spiced Pear Rolls with Warm Pear Caramel, 36
Classic Cinnamon Rolls, 24–25
coconut, 62–63
coffee
   Espresso-Chocolate Cinnamon Rolls with Cappuccino Drizzle, 41
Coffee Lover's Cinnamon Monkey Bread Rolls, 19

cranberries, 44–45

cream cheese, 24

    Carrot Cake Cinnamon Rolls
        with Pineapple-Cream
        Cheese Frosting, 68–69

    Gluten-Free Cream Cheese
        Frosting, 74

crème fraîche

    Pain au Chocolat Cinnamon
        Rolls with Cinnamon-Crème
        Fraîche Icing, 82, 85

    Tarte Tatin Cinnamon Rolls
        with Crème Fraîche, 52–53

crowns, 57

    Cinnamon-Blueberry Crowns,
        57

    Sweet Cheese and Cinnamon
        Streusel Crowns, 40

    Vegan Sweet Potato-
        Cinnamon Crowns with
        Bourbon Icing, 64

    Whole Wheat Pumpkin-Pecan
        Cinnamon Crowns, 66–67

D

dairy products, xiv. *See also
    specific dairy products*

Danish pastries, 79

    Cinnamon Bear Claws, 80–81

    Franzbrotchen, 84–85

    Korvapuusti, 83

    Pain au Chocolat Cinnamon
        Rolls with Cinnamon-Crème
        Fraîche Icing, 82, 85

Danish Pastry Dough, 10–12

détrempe (sweet yeast dough),
    10

dough, xii, 1

    baking, xviii

    buerrage, 10–12

    cutting, xvii

    Danish Pastry, 10–12

    détrempe, 10

    Easy Cinnamon Roll, 2

    filling, xvii

    forming, xvii

    Gluten-Free Cinnamon Roll, 9

    Honeybun, 3

    Hot Cross Bun, 3

    kneading, xvi, 2

    laminating, xvii

    mixing, xvi, 2

    No-Knead Cinnamon Roll, 5

    No-Knead Pumpkin Cinnamon
        Roll, 5

    rising, xvi–xvii

    rolling out, xvii

    Thin and Rich Cinnamon
        Strudel, 6

    Thin Strudel, 6

    Traditional Cinnamon Roll, 3

    Vegan Cinnamon Roll, 7

    Vegan Whole Wheat
        Cinnamon Roll, 8

    Whole Wheat Cinnamon
        Roll, 8

E

Easy Cinnamon Roll Dough, 2

easy cinnamon rolls, 5, 13

    Bacon-Brown Sugar Cinnamon
        Rolls, 16

    Coffee Lover's Cinnamon
        Monkey Bread Rolls, 19

    Pineapple Upside-Down
        Cinnamon Rolls, 15

    Rocky Road Cinnamon Rolls,
        17

    Szechuan Pepper Cinnamon
        Rolls with Fresh Ginger
        Glaze, 20–21

    Yummy Glazed Cinnamon
        Rolls, 14

Espresso-Chocolate Cinnamon
    Rolls with Cappuccino
    Drizzle, 41

F

Festive Cranberry-Orange
    Cinnamon Rolls, 44–45

Finland, ix

    Korvapuusti, 83

flavor extracts, xiv

flours, xiv

    measurement of, xvi

Franzbrotchen, 84–85

Frosted Gluten-Free Cinnamon
    Rolls, 74

Frosted Vegan Cinnamon Rolls,
    60

fruit, 26–27

    Carrot Cake Cinnamon Rolls
        with Pineapple-Cream
        Cheese Frosting, 68–69

    Cinnamon-Blueberry Crowns,
        57

    Cinnamon-Spiced Pear Rolls
        with Warm Pear Caramel, 36

Festive Cranberry-Orange Cinnamon Rolls, 44–45
Gluten-Free Banana Blueberry Rolls, 76–77
Gluten-Free Skillet Apple-Cinnamon Rolls, 75
Going Bananas Vegan Cinnamon Rolls, 61
Orange Cinnamon Rolls with Sweet Orange Drizzle, 30
Orange Frosted Vegan Whole Wheat Cinnamon Rolls, 71
Pineapple Upside-Down Cinnamon Rolls, 15
Tarte Tatin Cinnamon Rolls with Crème Fraîche, 52–53
Whole Wheat, Black Walnut, and Apple Cinnamon Rolls, 70

G
Germany, ix–x
Franzbrotchen, 84–85
gluten-free, 73
Frosted Gluten-Free Cinnamon Rolls, 74
Gluten-Free Banana Blueberry Rolls, 76–77
Gluten-Free Cinnamon Roll Dough, 9
Gluten-Free Cinnamon-Walnut Monkey Bread with Maple Drizzle, 78
Gluten-Free Cream Cheese Frosting, 74
Gluten-Free Skillet Apple-Cinnamon Rolls, 75
Going Bananas Vegan Cinnamon Rolls, 61

H
Hodgson Mill flour, xiv
Honeybun Dough, 3
Cinnamon Buns, 28–29
Hot Cross Bun Dough, 3
Cinnamon Hot Cross Buns, 37
hot roll mix, xiv
Easy Cinnamon Roll Dough, 2

I
Ibarra brand Mexican chocolate, 34
Indonesian cinnamon, xv

K
kingarthur.com, xiv, 8, 41
kanelbullar, 33
kneading dough, xvi, 2. *See also* no-knead
Korvapuusti, 83

L
laminating, xvii
liquid ingredients, warming of, xvi

M
maple syrup, 75
Gluten-Free Cinnamon-Walnut Monkey Bread with Maple Drizzle, 78

McCormick spices, xiv
Mexican Chocolate Cinnamon Rolls, 34–35
molasses, 58
Moroccan Cinnamon Rose Petal Crescents, 54–55

N
New England Sticky Buns, 38
No-Knead Cinnamon Roll Dough, 5
no-knead cinnamon rolls
Cardamom- and Cinnamon-Scented Swedish Tea Ring, 46–48
Espresso-Chocolate Cinnamon Rolls with Cappuccino Drizzle, 41
Festive Cranberry-Orange Cinnamon Rolls, 44–45
Sweet Cheese and Cinnamon Streusel Crowns, 40
No-Knead Pumpkin Cinnamon Roll Dough, 5
No-Knead Pumpkin-Cinnamon Pullaparts, 42–43
nuts. *See* pecans; walnuts

O
oil, cinnamon, 63
old-fashioned cinnamon rolls
Big-as-a-Plate Cinnamon Rolls with Gooey Frosting, 31
Cinnamon Honeybuns, 28–29
Cinnamon Hot Cross Buns, 37

old-fashioned cinnamon rolls
    (continued)
    Cinnamon-Spiced Pear Rolls
       with Warm Pear Caramel, 36
    Classic Cinnamon Rolls, 24–25
    Mexican Chocolate Cinnamon
       Rolls, 34–35
    New England Sticky Buns, 38
    Orange Cinnamon Rolls with
       Sweet Orange Drizzle, 30
    Schnecken, 26–27
    Swedish Cinnamon Rolls,
       32–33
Orange Cinnamon Rolls with
    Sweet Orange Drizzle, 30
Orange Frosted Vegan Whole
    Wheat Cinnamon Rolls, 71

P
Pain au Chocolat Cinnamon
    Rolls with Cinnamon-Crème
    Fraîche Icing, 82, 85
pantry, xiv–xv
pears
    Cinnamon-Spiced Pear Rolls
       with Warm Pear Caramel, 36
pecans
    New England Sticky Buns, 38
    Whole Wheat Pumpkin-Pecan
       Cinnamon Crowns, 66–67
penzeys.com, xiv
Pineapple Upside-Down
    Cinnamon Rolls, 15
Pioneer spices, xiv
povitica, 56

pumpkin
    No-Knead Pumpkin Cinnamon
       Roll Dough, 5
    No-Knead Pumpkin-Cinnamon
       Pullaparts, 42–43
    Whole Wheat Pumpkin-Pecan
       Cinnamon Crowns, 66–67

R
raisins, 26–27
rising, of dough, xvi–xvii
Rocky Road Cinnamon Rolls, 17
rolling out, xvii
rugelach, 50–51

S
Saigon cinnamon, xv
salt, xiv
Schnecken, 26–27
Slavic Cinnamon-Walnut Twists
    56
Small Indulgence Cinnamon
    Rolls, 58
sorghum syrup, 75
spices, xiv. *See also specific*
    spices
    baharat, 55
    flavor extracts, xiv
Sweden, ix
    Cardamom- and Cinnamon-
       Scented Swedish Tea Ring,
       46–48
Swedish Cinnamon Rolls, 32–33
Sweet Cheese and Cinnamon
    Streusel Crowns, 40

sweeteners, xiv
    maple syrup, 75, 78
    molasses, 58
    pearl sugar, xiii
    sorghum syrup, 75
Szechuan Pepper Cinnamon
    Rolls with Fresh Ginger
    Glaze, 20–21

T
Tarte Tatin Cinnamon Rolls with
    Crème Fraîche, 52–53
Thin and Rich Cinnamon Strudel
    Dough, 6
Thin Strudel Dough, 6
thin strudel dough cinnamon
    rolls, 49
    Cinnamon Rugelach, 50–51
    Moroccan Cinnamon Rose
       Petal Crescents, 54–55
    Slavic Cinnamon-Walnut
       Twists, 56
    Small Indulgence Cinnamon
       Rolls, 58
    Tarte Tatin Cinnamon Rolls
       with Crème Fraîche, 52–53
Tone's spices, xiv
Traditional Cinnamon Roll
    Dough, 3
    Big-as-a-Plate Cinnamon Rolls
       with Gooey Frosting, 31
    Cinnamon-Spiced Pear Rolls
       with Warm Pear Caramel, 36
    Classic Cinnamon Rolls, 24–25

Mexican Chocolate Cinnamon
Rolls, 34–35
New England Sticky Buns, 38
Orange Cinnamon Rolls with
Sweet Orange Drizzle, 30
Schnecken, 26–27
Swedish Cinnamon Rolls,
32–33

V
Vegan Cinnamon Roll Dough, 7
vegan cinnamon rolls, 59
Frosted Vegan Cinnamon
Rolls, 60
Going Bananas Vegan
Cinnamon Rolls, 61
Orange Frosted Vegan Whole
Wheat Cinnamon Rolls, 71
Vegan Coconut-Cinnamon
Pullaparts with Lime Glaze,
62–63
vegan products, xiv
Vegan Sweet Potato-Cinnamon
Crowns with Bourbon Icing,
64
Vegan Whole Wheat Cinnamon
Roll Dough, 8
Vietnamese cinnamon, xv
vital wheat gluten, xiv

W
walnuts
Gluten-Free Cinnamon-Walnut
Monkey Bread with Maple
Drizzle, 78

Slavic Cinnamon-Walnut
Twists, 56

Whole Wheat, Black Walnut,
and Apple Cinnamon Rolls,
70
whole wheat cinnamon rolls, 65
Carrot Cake Cinnamon Rolls
with Pineapple-Cream
Cheese Frosting, 68–69
Orange Frosted Vegan Whole
Wheat Cinnamon Rolls, 71
Whole Wheat, Black Walnut, and
Apple Cinnamon Rolls, 70
Whole Wheat Cinnamon Roll
Dough, 8
Whole Wheat Pumpkin-Pecan
Cinnamon Crowns, 66–67

X
xanthan gum, xiv

Y
yeast, xiv, xvi
Yummy Glazed Cinnamon Rolls,
14